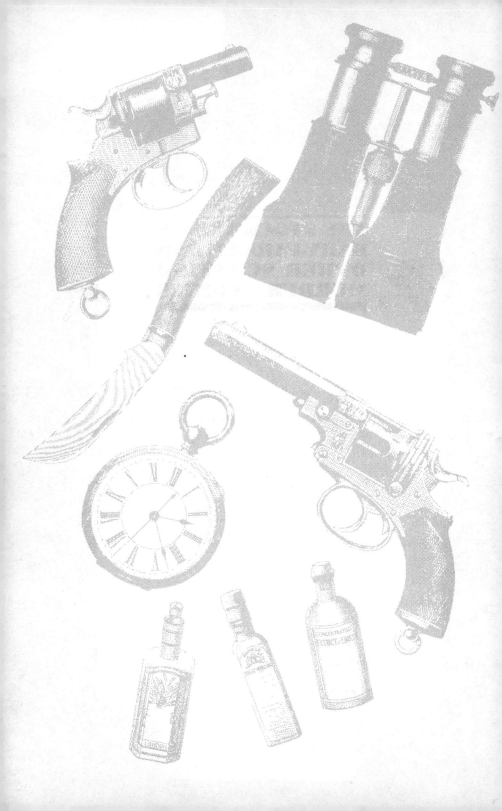

Molly Whittington-Egan

THE STOCKBRIDGE BABY-FARMER AND OTHER SCOTTISH MURDER STORIES

Neil Wilson Publishing • Glasgow • Scotland

Neil Wilson Publishing
303a The Pentagon Centre
36 Washington Street
GLASGOW
G3 8AZ
Tel: 0141-221-1117
Fax: 0141-221-5363
E-mail: info@nwp.sol.co.uk
http://www.nwp.co.uk/

ISBN 1-903238-05-6
Typeset in Bodoni
Designed by Mark Blackadder

Printed by WS Bookwell, Finland

ACKNOWLEDGEMENTS

My special thanks to
Hilary Bailey,
Glenn Chandler,
Max Falconer,
Dr Marc Hinchliffe,
Carole Hopkins,
John Linklater and
Richard Whittington-Egan

BY THE SAME AUTHOR

Khaki Mischief: The Agra Murder Case

Murder on the Bluff: The Carew Poisoning Case

Scottish Murder Stories

Jack l'Éventreur
(a translation of the novel by Jean Dorsenne)

Dr Forbes Winslow: Defender of the Insane

With Richard Whittington-Egan

The Story of Mr George Edalji (Ed.)

The Bedside Book of Murder

The Murder Almanac

CONTENTS

CHAPTER 1
THE STOCKBRIDGE BABY FARMER

One October afternoon in the Stockbridge district of Edinburgh, a group of young boys were larking around in Cheyne Street. There was a longish parcel, dirty, scuffed, lying out in the open on a bare, so-called 'green', and when they kicked it open, hoping for a lucky find, such as a discarded pair of boots, the dead body of a baby unrolled in front of them.

Scared, the boys ran for a policeman, and came back with Constable Stewart, who timed the report at 1.30pm, Friday, October 26th, 1888. He saw that the body was badly decomposed, and bore it off straight away to the city mortuary, where, the following day, Dr Henry Littlejohn examined the small corpse, which presented a mummified appearance, and was tightly wrapped in an oilskin coat. It was male, weighed 11lb 4oz and was 29 inches in length, and the child had been about one to one and a half years old, in good previous health. A ligature – an apron string, probably – had been applied twice around the neck, drawn hard, so that it was embedded in the skin. The only possible explanation for its presence was wilful strangulation.

Meanwhile, James Banks, a plasterer, who lived in Cheyne Street, had become suspicious on hearing of the discovery of a dead baby only 20 yards from his home. That June, he had let a room to a couple calling themselves Mr and Mrs Macpherson. They were allotted a coal-closet, which they kept locked. In September, Mrs Macpherson had driven up in a cab, one day, with a baby. Isabella Banks, the plasterer's daughter, had held it while Mrs Macpherson paid the cabman. She asked whose baby it was. It was a little girl, the lodger replied, and its mother would soon come for it. Then she threw it up in her arms in a fine gesture of benevolence and said, '*My bonnie wee bairn*!' That bairn was never seen alive again.

She told Mr Banks that she had got a child, and £25 to keep it, and had parted with it to a certain person for £18, leaving £7 for herself. We can be sure that, in the climate of the times, Banks would not have been surprised by the transaction, but rather by the speed of the transfer. Mrs Banks had been away from home during the month of September, and on her return, the family told her about the disappearing child. She asked Mrs Macpherson point-blank what had become of it and she said that she had put it away, and if a servant-girl came asking for her, she was to send her off, saying that she was in church.

Mrs Macpherson herself was pregnant, with the birth imminent. Mrs Banks noticed that there was a baby's hat on the bed, and asked why she had bought it in advance – which speaks volumes for the poor circumstances of these people, and the qualified expectation of a live, healthy birth. The story was that it was her niece's hat. She went away to have her baby and returned in due course without it. Once Mrs Banks asked her for the key of the coal-closet, and she refused, saying that she had dirty clothing in there. The Macphersons used a special chap (knock) when they let each other into the house.

James Banks, reflecting on these uncertain matters, decided to go to the police. Detective Clark, of Edinburgh City Police, heard his story and was very interested, although the little girl who had vanished was obviously not the boy found in the street. A very young female infant had been reported missing. Mrs Tomlinson, wife of Samuel Tomlinson, of 6 Wardrop's Court, Lawnmarket, had told the police that her daughter, Alice Tomlinson, a domestic servant, had given birth on August 11th to an illegitimate baby, Violet Duncan Tomlinson, in the Edinburgh Maternity Hospital. Alice was in no position to care for an infant. She, the mother, had taken Violet in, but only temporarily, while advertising for someone to adopt her.

Among a number of applicants, a Mrs Burns, of Cheyne Street, had submitted the lowest tender. She had said that she wanted the baby for her sister, Mrs Macpherson, who was married to the Duke of Montrose's piper, and would take the child to live in splendid country surroundings on the Duke's estate. This colourful fabrication was a clinching enticement, and Mrs Tomlinson had parted with Violet, aged one month, paying over a premium of £2 to Mrs Burns when she came to collect her. Since then, Mrs Tomlinson had gone several times to the house in Cheyne Street to see how her granddaughter was getting on, but had always been turned away and had begun to harbour doubts. Her daughter, Alice, had become ill, and was admitted to the Edinburgh Royal Infirmary.

Inspector Clark proceeded to Cheyne Street and cornered Mrs Macpherson *alias* Mrs Burns. He asked her what had become of Violet Tomlinson. She produced a pair of baby's shoes and a vaccination certificate (immunisation against smallpox being then compulsory) and stated that she was with her sister, who was married to the Duke of Montrose's piper. Unimpressed, the inspector searched the house and actually found the key of the coal-closet. The woman went to pieces, and begged him not to open the door. As he went forward to use the key, according to his supporting colleague, David Simpson, detective officer, she cried out, 'Get a cab! Take me to the police station. It is there. I did it!'

The door was unlocked and revealed a chamber of horrors. The corpse of a baby girl, wrapped in a canvas cloth, was lying on the bottom shelf. This was, in fact, Violet Tomlinson. On the top shelf, there was a stain corresponding to the shape of a child's body, together with some pieces of cloth similar to that encasing the parcelled body found outside, and a canister which had contained chloride of lime. Contrary to still-held popular belief, lime does not aid decomposition, but rather retards it, and soft tissues are largely preserved. If water is added, to slake quicklime, some mummification will occur. Here, chlorinated lime was probably used for its disinfectant properties, to lessen smell. On this shelf, the body of Alexander Gunn had lain before being used as a football. He was one of twins, and his brief history will be told a little later.

A quantity of children's clothing was also found in the house and the police officers were by now quite sure in their own minds that they had found the lair of a typical baby-farmer. The vile trade in unwanted babies, most often illegitimate, at a time when small value was placed on infant life, was not in itself illegal. The practice was called 'adoption' but it was really fostering, and there was no legal force to the transaction. Generally, it was the activity of very impoverished people. Desperate mothers, or their agents, handed over their children to slatterns who cared for them with such negligence and omissions that death often supervened, or, as the money that came with them ran out, resorted to deliberate murder. The baby-farmers did not 'buy' the children: it was the other way round. A child on weekly terms stood a better chance of survival than a baby taken with a lump sum. The deprivation of mother's milk and inadequate feeding with slops was often sufficient to ease the parting. If large numbers were taken in, the health problems multiplied.

Sometimes the babies passed down a chain of these 'carers' for lesser and lesser funds, the procedure known as 'baby-sweating'. The babies were lost, had no identity, and the last thing that the baby-farmers wanted was a parent trying to stay in touch with them, or the babies. They kept on the move, changed addresses, used *aliases*, and were proficient liars.

The spread of the railway system aided the transfer of babies in secrecy, under the station clock, before they were borne off, wrapped in their clean shawls, to a short and horrible future. Sedatives were used indiscriminately – laudanum was freely available – and weak and puny babies were stupefied with alcohol.

The problem was just as widespread in Scotland as in England. In 1870, the Glasgow-based *North British Daily Mail* ran its own enquiry into 'Baby-Farming in Scotland' and found many gross cruelties. As a result of an undercover approach, a terrible establishment was disclosed at a respectable-looking house near Arthur's Seat. There were whippings and mysterious disappearances. The colonies, such as New Zealand, where respectability ruled, were not immune. As social conditions improved, and legislation whittled away at the abuses, gradually there were alternatives to baby-farming. The NSPCC was founded in 1889. In blatant cases of outright murder, the police acted. By the time of the Cheyne Street discovery, there was beginning to be less tolerance by the public and the police. The last baby-farmer to be hanged in Britain was Leslie James, *alias* Rhoda Willis, in 1907.

Who knows how many adoptions this Mrs Macpherson had already conducted? She was probably in mid-career. Apprehended murdering baby-farmers showed a pattern of previous killings not admitted to, which might come to light years later. Further enquiries established that her real name was Jessie King. She was a wretched, undernourished creature, aged 27, yet with some vestige of that prerequisite of the successful baby-farmer – a respectable mien. She was a Roman Catholic. As so often there was a male partner or hanger-on. She was, of necessity, the front woman but behind her there lurked the suspicious figure of Thomas Pearson, *alias* Macpherson, her ancient lover of unprepossessing aspect, burly like a bear with a muddy grey-bearded face and a monstrous wen nestling in his bald pate. He called himself a labourer.

The police traced Jessie King's movements back one year to October, 1887, when she was living with Thomas Pearson at 24 Dalkeith Road. Pearson was the name on their door in the tenement and the noticeably older man was supposed to be her uncle. Sometimes the couple were known to be the worse for drink, and there were sounds of quarrelling. There came David Ferguson Finlay, of 16 Lindsay Place, Leith, that stock Victorian character, a seducer. He had impregnated a girl named Elizabeth Campbell and she had taken refuge at the home of her sister and brother-in-law, John Anderson, at High Street, Prestonpans, where, on May 20th, 1887, she had given birth to a boy – Walter Anderson Campbell. She herself had died one week later.

Her sister, Janet, left with the baby, told David Finlay that she would be willing to adopt Walter if he would pay 'aliment', but this would have been a continuing drain on his precious resources, and he preferred to make his own plans. Adoption advertisements, inserted by either party, i.e. by those offering a child or those seeking one, were carried even by high-class newspapers well into the 20th century. Finlay advertised his love-child on the open market, and Jessie King and Thomas Pearson, operating under the name of Stewart, with Pearson posing as Jessie's father, were chosen, Finlay contracting to pay the lump sum of £5 for Walter's continuing maintenance. He did visit and inspect the room at 24 Dalkeith Road, but then he considered his duty well done and made no further enquiries. He wrote a brief note to Janet Anderson at Prestonpans – 'a party will call for the child tomorrow forenoon'. That is how it was done. It was not, as we have said, illegal, but it was clandestine and it was shameful.

On August 20th, the oleaginous father and daughter called with their note of authorisation. The man conducted the arrangements and the woman had a tale to spin: she was a poor widow, and her baby of the same age as Walter had passed away and she had been depressed ever since. Off they went with the two-month-old baby, in perfect health, together with its birth certificate and vaccination paper, which was solemnly returned by post, filled up, and handed to the registrar by Janet Anderson. The pair had declined to give Janet their address but there was nothing she could do about that, except, presumably, ask David Finlay. At 24 Dalkeith Road, neighbours were aware that the Pearsons had a child about the place, but after three months it was no longer there – sent away to its aunt, as the explanation went – and Walter Campbell was never seen again, alive or dead.

The loving adopters moved on, and by March, 1888, were installed in a house in Ann's Court, Canonmills. Their next target was, typically, a domestic servant, Catherine Gunn. On May 1st, 1887, at 54 Bristo Street, she had been delivered of the unwelcome gift of twin sons, who were illegitimate. After four days, they had been put with a Mrs Henderson, of 17 Rose Street, who had looked after them very well, for weekly payment, but Catherine could not go on like that forever. There was not even a David Finlay in evidence. She had had to work again, or starve. Small wonder that quite a number of live-born babies were passed off as stillborn. There were a few philanthropic institutions which took in babies, but there were not enough places to go round. 'Adoption' was the only solution for mothers like Catherine.

Nearly a year had passed, and, defeated, she had asked Mrs Euphemia Mackay, a monthly nurse or unqualified midwife, who had attended her in her confinement, to insert one of the infamous advertisements, seeking a permanent adopter. There was always a chance that a genuine home might be found. There were 29 replies, which indicated that the trade in babies was still thriving. Most of those replies, it appears, will have contained false claims of the ideal conditions awaiting a dear little baby.

You would have thought that the twins could have gone as a pair, but Robert probably did better than Alexander, because Jessie King got him, on April 5th with the princely sum of £2. He was small, but 'strong to be a twin' and in normal health. The intermediary nurse called twice at Ann's Court, and was satisfied with Alexander's progress. Mr and Mrs Macpherson, as the kindly couple styled themselves, seemed very fond of the child, and called him Sandy. A little girl, Janet Burnie, of 6 Front Baker's Land, Canonmills, was paid a pittance to care for Sandy for long hours – from 10am to 6pm. She did nothing wrong. On one occasion, Mrs Elizabeth Mackenzie, Jessie King's landlady, objected when she saw Jessie 'pouring whisky over the baby's throat'. Sandy's mother, relieved of her burden, got married, and lived happily at 6 Huntly Street, Canonmills.

In May, 1888, Sandy was suddenly no longer there. Jessie said that his mother had died in the Royal Infirmary, and another woman had taken him. However, she also told Janet Burnie that his father had come during the night and taken him away. The little girl then went to 'Mr Macpherson' for an explanation, and was told that the child was away across the water, for the good of his health. This was the baby found in Cheyne Street with an apron string tied round its neck, after Jessie moved there in June.

Since there was strong suspicion of three child murders, Jessie King and Thomas Pearson were arrested, but Jessie entirely exonerated her paramour in her judicial declaration and he was released to bear witness for the Crown against her. He was immune from prosecution, although his shared guilt was obvious. Jessie King alone was put to her capital trial at the High Court of Justiciary in Edinburgh on February 18th, 1889, charged with murdering Walter Campbell, aged five months, Alexander Gunn, 12 months, and Violet Tomlinson, six weeks.

Thomas Pearson gave his perfidious evidence under the staring gaze of Jessie King in the dock. He knew nothing about any killings, he said. The sums got with the children were all spent properly on the household expenses. He admitted that he had gone under three names: Pearson, Stewart and Macpherson. He had used the latter ever since he was a boy. He had found it an appropriate name when he was attending the Highland gatherings. His name could be seen in the *Scotsman* in 1857, as the winner of a first-class prize. He certainly did help to adopt Walter Campbell from Prestonpans, because Jessie wanted a child. After three weeks, it was missing, and Jessie said that she had grown tired of it and taken it to Miss Stirling's Home: '*he would see the boy running about the Causeway with a blue gown on.*'

Evidence was brought that there was a home so named in Stockbridge, not Causewayside, and that Walter Anderson Campbell was not on the registers. He had simply vanished. The police and Dr Littlejohn had twice searched the premises at 24 Dalkeith Road and were satisfied that the body was not there, after taking up the flooring of two houses and examining the coal cellars of both. In fact, the Crown was soon to withdraw the charge relating to this child. Cunningly, Jessie King had refused throughout to say anything at all about him.

As for the twin, Alexander Gunn, or Sandy, Jessie had kept him for three weeks and he remembered coming home one night and finding him gone. Jessie said that she had taken him to Miss Stirling's. He had wanted to visit Sandy there, but Jessie said that male visitors were not admitted. He had no knowledge of Jessie's bringing a baby girl (Violet Tomlinson) to Cheyne Street, nor did he know whether or not the coal-closet in the passage was kept locked. His oilskin coat had disappeared and Jessie had said that she had thrown it out because it was covered in green mould. He thought that was a pity.

Jessie King's declaration, read out, caused horror in court. It contained graphic admissions and also classic baby-farmers' lies and evasions. She *did* try to get the twin, Sandy, into Miss Stirling's Home, and others, but all refused because he was illegitimate. Thomas Pearson loved the little boy so, but they were poor people and could not afford to keep it. One Monday after she had unsuccessfully tried to place the child, she had drunk too much and lied to Pearson that she was off to Miss Stirling's. He went out and while he was away, she strangled the boy and put him in a cupboard. When they moved to Cheyne Street, she took the body with her, in a box and then hid it in the coal-closet. Later, she put the body outside.

As for Violet Tomlinson, the adoption was all her own work and Pearson had nothing to do with it. She brought the baby home while he was away at his work, and gave it some whisky to keep it quiet. The spirits were stronger than she had thought and took the baby's breath away. While it lay gasping, she put her hand on its mouth and choked it. When it was dead, she put the body in the closet where it lay until the police found it. She had tied a cloth over its mouth in case it came alive while she was out, and made a noise. (Her account was not in accordance with the post-mortem findings of Dr Henry Littlejohn and Dr Joseph Bell, who, while noting that the lower part of the face was, indeed, tightly enveloped in a piece of cotton cloth, twisted at the back of the head and knotted at the throat, found that the actual cause of death was strangulation by a ligature round the neck. Such was a favoured method of the baby-farmers: Mrs Amelia Elizabeth Dyer boasted, 'You'll know mine by the tape around their necks.')

There was a view, which took little cognizance of the human suffering involved, that the mothers of children offered for adoption connived at their eventual demise. If that were so, the money scraped together at what cost to go with the child must have represented a conscience-salving device! Closing for the defence, Counsel tried this approach, suggesting that the parents were not without their share of moral responsibility. However, the grief of Sandy's mother in the witness box as she identified a pair of baby's shoes was well remarked and it was remembered that she had paid weekly terms for the twins to be properly cared for until they were nearly one year old.

Was it not possible, Counsel suggested, as he had to, that Jessie King had been under the influence and control of Thomas Pearson throughout and was acting as much for his advantage as her own? He asked for a verdict of culpable homicide, but he did not prevail, because the case was beyond mercy. Baby-farmers, like serial killers, were not prone to remorse. They were too hardened, being, if we must define, mass killers for gain. Once they were caged, however, the tears flowed – for themselves. Mrs Dyer tried to throttle herself with her bootlaces, and Jessie King attempted strangulation in the condemned cell, with strips torn from her skirt. On March 11th, 1889, Jessie King became the last woman to be hanged in Edinburgh. The fate of her own baby, one of the lost children of the Victorian underworld, passed from hand to hand, or worse, was never revealed.

CHAPTER 2
'I AM GALL'

The smart way to approach the Peter Queen mystery – the classic discussion case – must be with temperance, not in the spirit of Sir Bernard Spilsbury, who was liable to stalk off in high dudgeon, refusing to speak to fellow-experts after a trial in which, as here, the jury did not believe him. Appearing unusually for the defence, he held to his adamantine opinion that suicide, not murder by Peter Queen, was the explanation for the death of his common-law wife, Chrissie Gall, on November 20th or 21st, 1931.

Had Queen strangled her, driven beyond endurance by her difficult, drunken behaviour, on an impulse, perhaps, or had she felt, indeed, in Gerard Manley Hopkins' searing words, that 'I am gall, I am heartburn. God's most deep decree/ Bitter would have me taste' and decided to end it all, on an impulse, perhaps?

It was regarded by those who had the conduct of the matter as a most difficult case, full of mysteries at every turn. The verdict of Not Proven was widely expected. The learned judge suggested, in terms, that the opposing medical experts cancelled one another out. The defence resented that comment. Professor Sidney Smith, called by the defence, felt that the facts did not warrant a definite opinion either way. The judge directed the jury to the circumstantial evidence in preference to the scientific views.

The scene of crime, strikingly photographed with only the bedclothes over the corpse altered by the investigators by folding back, should have been more productive of non-equivocal clues. The place was number 539 Dumbarton Road, Partick, Glasgow, that being a 'house' in a tenement, 'two stairs up', of a superior type, with a 'room' as well as a kitchen, both small. There is an extant plan, from an exhibit in court, showing the disposition of the furniture in the kitchen, which, typically was the actual, warmer living area, with bed recess, kitchen range, sink, four chairs, a table, two 'carpets', and a luxury – a gramophone cabinet.

This is by no means, unless the camera lies, a sordid setting for a sudden death. The wallpaper, which extends around the bed recess, is flower-sprigged, the valance of curtaining below the bed has a decorative border, the upper curtain, pulled back, is of some shiny material, and the bed-clothing is ample and comfortable. On the table in the foreground, which nearly abuts the bed, except for an upright chair set closely in the runnel between bed and table, there is a pale tablecloth with a hint of seersucker. Two potted plants, one of which looks remarkably like an aspidistra, and some remnants of a meal lie on the table: closest to the head of the bed, there is a shiny, rectangular tray bearing a plate with some discarded food to one side, of the consistency of mince or Christmas pudding. Other items visible are a large jug, probably for milk, a sugar bowl, a tall jar of relish type, two glasses, three cups and saucers with two of the cups not on their saucers, three spoons, one knife, and perhaps another, a small cluster of pearly bead-like objects, like a Christmas bauble or an ornament, an ashtray with one or two butts sticking up and an opened packet of cigarettes. It is impossible to see if there are any cigarettes left. The indications are not of a home where all hope had been abandoned.

There are no signs of a struggle on the bed or in the room. The young, slim body of Chrissie Gall lies on the outer side of the double bed (her usual place) half on her back, but with her legs drawn up and turned towards the wall. On the well-plumped up, very white pillow, her head is still neatly coiffed with a lacy cap, variously described as a mob-cap or a boudoir cap. Its purpose was, I believe, to preserve the hairstyle of the '30s. On the other pillow, to her left, apparently placed in an upright position, slanting at an angle of 45 degrees to the floor, is a bottle, nowhere designated, but almost certainly designed to hold alcohol. It looks as if some hand has deliberately planted it there. It may be full or empty or at some stage in-between.

The body is fully clothed in a garment, which, although said to be pyjamas looks more like a spangled, shiny kimono. It is not the bedtime apparel of a woman who has given up. Chrissie cared about appearances and there is a sad, jazz-age glamour about her death-bed. It is a famous photograph, and rightly so.

The house in Partick was a love-nest, of sorts, but really a sham, lacking in joy and romance. The relationship was fundamentally marred by Chrissie's heavy drinking and profound depressions. The doomed young couple had been secretly living in sin, at a time when the wedding ring mattered. She desperately wished to be taken as a married woman, which may explain her careful housekeeping, even though she was often incapacitated – unless Peter Queen saw to everything. He was quite capable of doing so. His inability to make a respectable woman of her, because he already had a living wife, was blamed for her poor mental state. All who observed the pair commented on his absolute devotion to her.

Peter Queen was born in Glasgow at the turn of the century to a life outwardly promising enough but mined with terrible unhappiness waiting for him to grow towards it. He was powerless, predestined. The son of a bookmaker, he worked for him as a clerk. At 19, he entered into a marriage and there was one son, but it was a failure, and the couple separated after only two years. He paid maintenance. In 1929, his wife was removed to Gartloch Mental Asylum. Her diagnosis was said to be chronic alcoholism, but I would not vouch for it.

The son was cared for by relatives.

Queen himself was later seen by two psychiatric experts, and they concluded that he was hypersensitive and nervous, and that his margin of control was exceedingly small. Since he was condemned to death at the time, this may not be a fair assessment. Of the several who have written on the case, none seems, other than William Roughead, although even he relegates the information to a footnote, to appreciate the importance of his special knowledge: 'I happen to know on high authority that he suffered from a minor form of epilepsy, *with short periods of unconsciousness.* [Author's italics.] Some years earlier he had tried to commit suicide by shooting himself through the left breast with a revolver, "because he had been blamed for losing a pair of boxing-gloves".'

The two doctors referred to above also stated that Queen had been taking bromide and chloral for a long time, as prescribed by his medical advisers. They do not specify the complaint, but those drugs were the medicament of choice for epilepsy in the '30s. It was not until a memorial pleading for his reprieve was presented that his illness was brought forward. As we shall see, his epilepsy might well explain parts of his conduct before and after the death. It will be only a suggestion.

In 1925, Queen first met Christina Gall, who was born in 1903, when she came to his home to work as a nursemaid for his younger siblings. She left school at 14 and went out in service as a housemaid. Her family were described as respectable, and she certainly feared their disapproval. Love bloomed. In October, 1927, her mother died and she went home to look after her father for three years, while still seeing Peter Queen, who took her out regularly in his car. Mr John Gall took a moderate view: 'I had made up my mind that nobody would be able to separate them; they seemed to be so much attached and had been meeting so long, that I thought it was impossible.'

Chrissie's drinking began after the death of her mother, which underlines the strong depressive element associated with her alcoholism. I wonder, however, if her decision to leave the Queen household after two years, in order to keep house for her father was not in fact motivated by filial duty but rather arose out of a desire to use the opportunity to cause some kind of change or resolution of a deadlocked relationship? Now, as Queen still pursued her, her behaviour deteriorated. She spent her household allowance on drink and failed to pay the rent. She was nearly 30 and she had no prospects.

By September, 1930, Mr Gall had had enough and he decided to wind up the house and go to live with a married daughter. Chrissie was homeless, her position was insecure and she was a liability, but Queen did not abandon her. On the same night that she left her father's roof, he transported her to live as a lodger with his friends, James and Fay Burns, at Hayburn Street. He was a tram conductor. They welcomed her and looked after her like a daughter. She was drunk when she arrived, and Mrs Burns put her to bed.

That Christmas, 1930, Queen left home and joined her in her lodgings. They lived as husband and wife, and Chrissie wore a wedding ring, telling the Burns' that Peter's wife had died, but it was too late, she was damaged and dejected and the drink had taken a vicious hold. She sneaked bottles into the house and hid them. Her days were idle and bleak when Peter was out at work. She herself was incapable of holding down a job. Having a baby was not an option. Alcohol is a depressant and she was seen to be 'at it' nearly all the time. When she was under the influence, she was awkward and quarrelsome, and then 'very low'.

Threats of suicide began to occur, although the Burns' did not tell Queen about them, thinking, perhaps, that they were only sick fancies, and not wishing to worry him. Sitting by the fire one day in a state of agitation, she suddenly made for the door, announcing that she was going to 'make a hole in the Clyde'. Mrs Burns prevented her and put her to bed. She was always being put to bed. '*Some day some of you will come in and find me strung up!*' she threatened when scolded for breaking her vain promises to reform.

'The gas' is always a problem in these situations. You don't put a kettle on the unlit gas if you intend to kill yourself, but you could, I suppose, be heedless that it was there, or you could even be overtaken by suicidal impulse in the very act of preparing to make a pot of tea. It was probably an accident, and a dangerous one, when Mr and Mrs Burns smelt gas in the middle of the night and found the gas ring in the kitchen full on under the kettle. At 2.00am, Fay Burns went to her lodgers' room to complain – 'She has just about gassed us all' – and found them *arguing* – a rare glimpse. Normally, in his small, private, domestic hell, Queen was seen to be ever kind, patient, and affectionate, quick to excuse and hide Chrissie's faults. This time, he said that he had been chasing her about all night and turning off the gases. He had found her in the lavatory with the gas full on and unlighted.

Mr Burns came to the conclusion that the relationship was absolutely hopeless, and advised Peter Queen to finish it and make Chrissie an allowance, even leave the country if that was the only way to extricate himself. Queen refused: he loved her and would never give her up. This was surely the ultimate declaration of regard, when another had offered him and as it were sanctioned an escape route. It was, though, high time to try a change of scene. No one has ever suggested that with extreme premeditation he deliberately transferred her to a more isolated setting where she was at his mercy – as can happen.

In August, 1931, the couple moved to their new house at 539 Dumbarton Road. There was no Fay Burns to supervise Chrissie during the day, and she was not a prisoner, continuing to go out to obtain alcohol by some means, and to visit relatives when she was sober enough. She kept up her practice of going to see her father and sisters every Wednesday, pretending that she was well placed in service in Kelvinside, and that was her day off. Queen rationed her household allowance to £3 per week, and she was supposed to keep up the rent of £2 per month. No alcohol was allowed in the house except for an occasional gill (quarter-pint) of whisky for social purposes. A supportive team of Mr and Mrs Burns, and other friends, Mr and Mrs Leonard Johnston (she being a sister of Fay Burns) kept an eye on Chrissie, coming in with bracing words.

A fortnight before the end there was an actual, unambiguous suicide attempt, unless Queen, who said that he witnessed it, was lying, and unless Mr and Mrs Burns were also lying. Chrissie herself, according to the Burns', heard them all discussing the incident and did not deny it. James and Fay Burns were invited to tea. As the husband went to hang his coat behind the kitchen door, he said, he noticed that the peg was broken. 'Who has been breaking up the happy little home?' he jested with a remarkable lack of tact. Peter said that it must have happened during the night (with the meaning that he did not know it was broken) when Chrissie had tried to do herself in. There is a rather strange nonchalance about his response, or perhaps embarrassment. Chrissie, who was in the kitchen, heard this exchange and merely remarked that she was a damn fool and was going to make an effort to stop the drinking.

Howsoever they all made light of it at the tea-party, the happening that night, if it did take place, had been truly appalling. Queen speaks: 'I was sleeping and was wakened up with a noise. I did not see anybody in bed, and I then got up and lit the gas to see what the noise was. I saw Chris sagging at the knees against the door, and I saw the two ropes, with a rope twisted round her neck. I immediately got her up as quickly as I could and took the rope off her neck. When I got her straightened up she fell against me, and I could see she was very much dazed. I put her to bed. I did not know what to do, but I got some water and moistened her lips, and I got into bed and stayed with her there and got her to be as quiet as I possibly could.'

Two days later, on November 14th, Leonard Johnston called and found Chrissie alone and perfectly sober. It seemed like a good time to reason with her: 'Chrissie, why not try to stop this drink? 'It is doing you harm.' He had excellent recall of her response, an outburst: 'Don't I know that? But do you understand the position I am in? Do you understand the pretension (*sic*) of it all? I am fed up with life. I have to tell lies everywhere I go. I cannot go home to my own people but I have got to tell lies. *Some day Peter will find me behind the door*.' She talked to Johnston about Peter: he adored her, had given her a coat, a beautiful ring, and the gramophone. She did not say how much she adored Peter.

Worried, he said, about Chrissie's threats of suicide, Queen arranged a holiday, which, although presumably well-meant, could only have made her worse. It was mid-winter, and on Monday, 23rd, she was to be shipped off to bracing Aberdeen, where he had taken rooms for her with friends who would look after her. A medical opinion would surely have been more advisable, but his head, if he was genuine, was firmly embedded in the sand. Nessie, a niece, who had not been well, was to be her companion, although just a child, in the mistaken idea that a dependant other would be a therapeutic influence. Chrissie hated the whole plan, too passive with the weight of her illness to want to leave the warm haven of her small home, but too low to resist.

Thursday, November 19th, was the day before she died. It was a misspent time, bibulous, oblivious, surprisingly egged on by her own brother, Robert, who drank glass for glass with her. Perhaps he had no real knowledge of her problem. What it shows is that she was incorrigible, coming to the end of the road, and that Peter Queen would have had to be some kind of saint – perhaps he was – not to be disillusioned. After Peter had gone to work, she went to see her father, also at work, to tell him about Aberdeen, but he was too busy to talk, and they arranged to meet the following evening at her married sister's home. We can see how dependent Chrissie still was on her own family, and they, incidentally, suspicious no doubt of Peter Queen, were to be anxious to play down the seriousness of Chrissie's illness.

After being somewhat rebuffed by her father, she proceeded instead to visit the married sister, Mrs Walker, at her house in Shettleston Road, where she also found Robert Gall, not at work. Her handbag contained whisky and a bottle of beer. The telegram from Aberdeen which confirmed her booking was produced. Drinking took place. At 5.00pm, brother and sister left. She was unsteady. They went to a nearby public house, where she downed two small whiskies, a bottle and a glass of beer, and a large port. Robert gave her best on the port. As a takeaway, she stowed a gill of whisky in her handbag. Robert thought that he ought to escort her home – the secret, shameful home to which no member of her family had been admitted.

In Dumbarton Road there was a last, tempting bar, but the waiter refused to serve them, objecting that the lady had had enough. Chrissie told him what she thought of him. Peter Queen was waiting on the landing when they reached number 539. It was 9.15, and Chrissie had promised to be back at 5.15. She lied an alcoholic's lie, and said that she had been all that time at her sister's. In a touching scene which just might have been rank hypocrisy, although the mind rejects the idea, Queen lit the fire, took off Chrissie's wet shoes, and dried her feet. He put the kettle on for tea and brought a half bottle of White Horse whisky from a cupboard. All three had a small glass. Chrissie passed Queen a note. He acted on it, saying to Robert, 'You see, Bert, this is my aunt's house. I will have to

get a move on, as Chris has a good bit to go to get home.'
Playing along, Robert politely announced, 'I think I will need
to be going before the aunt comes in.' Queen saw him to his
car.

Chrissie was inconsolable about this incident, according to
Peter Queen, blaming herself for letting it happen, revealed as
a kept woman. And so she went to bed, with only the spectacle
of the ordeal in Aberdeen ahead of her. The next morning,
Friday, November 20th, she dragged her tottery body out of
bed, dressed, and went out. At 1.00pm she rang Queen at his
office from a public telephone and asked him to go home
because she felt ill. He was back by 2.00pm, and found Mrs
Johnston already there. She considered Chrissie to be very
drunk, and left, advising him to get a doctor. At 4.00pm, she
returned with her husband. Chrissie was in bed, asleep. They
left. What was Queen doing all this time? Thinking, smoking,
doing the housework? Leonard Johnston came back at
7.00pm. Chrissie was still asleep. He told Queen that he had
just seen the doctor's car outside his surgery, so that he was
available. Queen went off, but, he said, the doctor was
inundated with patients, so he left a message for him to make
a house call the following morning.

Johnston went home. Mrs Johnston popped back at 8
o'clock, to relieve Queen of his watch. Leonard and Peter had
a game of cribbage and two small whiskies and two half-pints
of beer in the Windsor Bar. What relevance this episode holds
must be grasped for; it seems to show that life was still going
on, that Queen was bearing up well, not in despair, supported
by kind friends. Mrs Johnston, who always took the firmest
stand on Chrissie's drinking, was in charge. Soon after 8
o'clock, she woke up, *stupid with drink.* She did not know
where she was and asked if Mrs Johnston would go for a gill of
whisky. This was refused, her friend saying that she had
brought some, which of course she had not: she did find some
whisky in the house, and gave Chrissie just a very little with

hot water and sugar. She went to sleep again.

The two men were soon back, between 9.00 and 10.00pm. Chrissie was now awake and taking notice. With his usual solicitude, Queen ascertained that she had had nothing to eat. Tea was made. He propped her up on the pillows and put on her dressing-jacket and cap, for decency. There she sat, presiding, swaying a little, in disgrace, poorly, yet still functioning and able to chime into the conversation. A kind of picnic took place, a communal effort, informed at least on some fronts by kindness and even enjoyment of the bizarre occasion.

'By Jove! This knife is blunt,' quoth Leonard Johnston, sportingly sawing away at a loaf for sandwiches.

'Peter, give him the right knife,' Chrissie told him, and Queen took the knife to her bedside to demonstrate that it was in fact the actual bread knife. She looked at the implement which was, so soon, to be a part of the apparatus of her death – according to the Crown. Hungry, she ate some sandwiches, and, rather sad to relate, asked for more. Queen gave her his own portion, since there was no bread left.

The visitors went home at 10.45pm. Mrs Johnston said that Chrissie was still stupid with drink, helpless, and unable to walk about. Mr Johnston thought the she *could* have got up and walked. Anyway, she would surely have needed to go to the lavatory, even if supported by Queen. Johnston's considered opinion was that there was a distinct improvement in her condition when he left, compared with her incapable state at 4 o'clock in the afternoon.

So it was midnight, and there she lay, knowing that the doctor was calling in the morning, and hoping, perhaps that he would say that she ought not to go to Aberdeen. She was going to see her father in the evening. People had been looking after her. There was food in her stomach. She had not had a real drink since the morning, just the little nip at 8 o'clock. It may be that she now slipped out of bed and found some more whisky.

The neighbours who lived above and below heard no

disturbance all night long, but a man who lived directly above said that he heard male voices talking in the Queens' kitchen. This is most mysterious, unless, of course, he was mistaken. Peter Queen could have been talking to another visitor, unexpected, or one brought in by Queen to help and advise.

The hours passed, and then at 2.45am Queen was seen in Crawford Street, near Dumbarton Road, where he asked a constable on his beat to direct him to the nearest police office. You would think that he would know, after ten weeks in the district. He was directed to Partick Police Office, where he arrived at 3.00am in a very agitated state and placed two house keys on the counter, saying, 'Go to 539 Dumbarton Road; I think you will find my wife dead.' Two experienced police officers were on night duty. Three times they asked him what was wrong. Then, they swore, Peter Queen uttered the fatal words, 'I think I have killed her.'

At his trial, in due course, Queen insisted that his actual words had been, *'Don't think I have killed her.'* I am sorry to say that, to a lawyer, the neat, exonerative substitution of one vital word for another immediately arouses scepticism. It is a well-known device employed by accused persons. Queen had no criminal record, but, working as he did for a Glasgow bookmaker, he must have been no innocent. However, it was greatly in his favour that, as only disclosed at the trial under close questioning by the judge, Lord Alnes, the officers on duty had not recorded the so-called confession in writing.

Two constables hastened to the address and used the keys. There, gas was lit in the kitchen. The body was lying underneath the bedclothes, which were pulled up chest-high. The left arm lay stretched out across the bed, on top of the bedclothes. The right arm, beneath the clothes, was bent at the elbow and the hand lay against the right hip, with the fingers flexed. A piece of cord was tied very tightly around the neck with a half knot (i.e. the first loop of a reef-knot) in front of the throat, below the Adam's apple, nearly central, slightly to the right of the middle line. The ends of the cord, which were of equal length, were *below* the bedclothes. Constable McGuffie undid the knot and loosened the cord, revealing a red mark round the neck.

Dr Christie, police surgeon, sent for at once, arrived at 5.00am, and his opinion was that death by strangulation had taken place about three hours previously – that is, about one hour before Queen had reported the death. The cord, which was three feet long, had been cut from the dangling loop used to hoist up and down the clothes pulley or airer, that contraption of long wooden slats slotted into metal brackets which was still in use far into the century and has recently been revived as an arty-crafty accessory. It was the same cord which, if it really happened, Chrissie had used *in situ* to hang herself behind the door. The cleat on which the loop was fastened was fixed actually on the door, which was only two feet from the foot of the bed.

Dr Christie found the face placid, with no expression of pain. The upper dentures were still in place. The tongue protruded half an inch from the mouth. Meanwhile, the constables had telephoned back what they had found and Peter Queen was brought to the bar, cautioned, and charged with murder. Why, it was afterwards well asked, would they have taken that swift action if the police had not been under the impression that he had confessed? 'I have nothing to say' was his response. He nearly collapsed, asked for water, which was brought before removal to an observation cell. The two pathologists who performed a post-mortem at Partick mortuary the next day were responsible for a bad mistake by omission. There was some fluid in the stomach (which was intensely congested) and, without further enquiry, the doctors contented themselves with the finding that there was no smell of alcohol. A vital point, which required specificity, had not been cleared up. If Chrissie had been stupid with drink, it would have been easier to overpower her. In the alternative, she would not have been in a fit state to kill herself.

The cricoid cartilage below the voice-box, not the hyoid bone which we usually hear about in these cases, was cracked or broken, depending on your terminology. The face was blotched and suffused. The absence of solid food in the stomach accords with the last meal of sandwiches at 9.00pm which would have been absorbed by 1.00am, one hour before the estimated time of death.

By the time that Peter Queen was brought to the High Court of Justiciary in Glasgow on January 5th, 1932, he had recovered himself and stood up straight to give evidence in his own defence. Sir Bernard Spilsbury and Dr Sidney Smith were engaged for him. He had plenty to say, but there were gaps and weaknesses. It was not a defence that was pat, streamlined. Going back to the Friday when she summoned him home, he found Chrissie leaning against the sink, crying, hysterical and under the influence of drink. He put her to bed, changed the linen, and gave her a hot-water bottle.

After their visitors had left, Chrissie seemed to want to talk, and they did so for an hour. She was worried about her family's new knowledge of her situation – if Robert divulged it – and she was worried about the holiday. She did not want to go away and had nothing packed. When he told her that the doctor would be calling, she asked him to look in the room for the best, embroidered pillow-slips, even though he had already changed the linen earlier in the afternoon. (I suppose it was verified that he did make the medical appointment?) This does seem to be a very understandable and feminine request which only a particularly cunning man could have made up. It is also, incidentally, not the request of a desperate woman planning suicide, or incubating that idea.

He went next door and searched for 15 minutes, but could not find the pillow-slips in the drawers. The room was dim because the gas in there gave a poor light – as verified by the police officers at the scene. He had to use matches. This part of his evidence was scoffed at. However, ask most husbands to go and find something domestic in another room, and they will fail. I have tested this premise on my friends. He was not clear, quite vague, about where he had found the bed-linen for the total change in the afternoon: 'As far as I know I would get them from the long drawer in the wardrobe...'

Then, he said, he went back into the kitchen and told Chrissie that he could not find the slips. There was no reply and he thought that she must be asleep. The defence case was that Chrissie Gall had employed that quarter of an hour while she was on her own to cut the cord, get back into bed and finish herself off. I suppose it could be suggested that she did not guess that it would take Peter so long to find the slips, and that she hoped to be saved, as she had been before. Or she could have sent him off on a fool's errand, knowing that the slips were not there, in order to give herself time.

After smoking a cigarette by the fire, he approached the bed and pulled the curtains to see if she was sleeping soundly so that he could get in without annoying her. It was then that he saw the rope round her neck and her face swollen. 'Chris! Chris! Chris!' he shouted, and he shook her. How can we be sure that Queen did not tamper with the body, the bedclothes or the cord? He did not seem to know what he did, being 'so shocked and absolutely knocked out'. He never improved upon the missing period of shock and collapse. Would he not, if full of guile and intent upon perjury, have invented any number of reasons for his delay in seeking help? Nor does he seem to realize that the one hour's conversation with Chrissie and the 15-minute search and the one cigarette bring him only to about midnight which is two whole hours before she died.

We may well imagine that his lawyers in preparation for trial pressed him hard to account for the missing periods. Is it possible that his epilepsy came over him and he was clinically confused, slumped in a chair in the room without full cognizance of time? Finding the body would have further confused him, which could explain his failure to remove the cord, his going to the police as if with guilty mind, afraid, as he said, of being blamed, and there giving an inappropriate account of himself.

The medical evidence was fiercely fought but, as was acknowledged, inconclusive. For the Crown, it was put that fracture of the cricoid had been recorded in only one case, and that was homicide, not suicide. The position of the dead woman's hands showed that she had not held the cord. However, it was conceded that a double knot would have been expected if murder had been committed. There should have been some defensive marks, unless the victim had been asleep. Unconsciousness would have supervened, in a suicide, before sufficient force had been exerted to break the cricoid and produce the deep indentation.

Said Professor Allison, 'I cannot conceive of a woman strangling herself and then placing her right arm underneath the bedclothes, arranging the bedclothes in an orderly fashion over her body, and leaving the ends of the cord tucked under the top of the bedclothes.' Dr Glaister said that unless the cord was held by another, the violent effort to breathe would tend to loosen the twist for it was not a complete knot, and the cord was relatively not hard.

For the defence, Sir Bernard Spilsbury had a peculiar theory about the half knot, which his colleague, Professor Sidney Smith, felt unable to go along with: it was to the effect that, as confirmed under the microscope, the fibres tended to bite into one another where they crossed and would hold the knot tight enough after Chrissie Gall's grip had relaxed. The actual position of the knot was one natural for suicide. There was an absence of haemorrhage and bruising in the deeper tissues of the neck and thyroid which indicated a lesser degree of force. Spilsbury admitted that he personally knew of no case of suicidal strangulation in a woman, or of a recorded instance of fracture of the cricoid in suicidal strangulation.

It might be of interest to cite the comment in Taylor's *Medical Jurisprudence*, revised by Sir Sidney Smith in 1956, on simulated suicidal strangulation: it would 'require great skill and premeditation on the part of a murderer so to dispose of the body of his victim, or to place it in such a relation to surrounding objects, as to cause real suspicion of suicide.' Peter Queen hardly fits this picture of cool cunning.

The suggestion that it was a kind of mercy-killing murder was not formally promulgated, although it was felt by commentators that Queen could realistically have feared that the doctor's visit could have led to admission to an asylum. Long-suffering as he was, he must have fought against the increasing possibility that a second woman connected to him was to be put away. He must have felt guilt, blamed himself: it would have been abnormal not to do so.

The bread knife is a serious flaw in the suicide argument. Johnston used it to cut the sandwiches. Queen said in cross-examination that he never touched it that night. So who put it back where it was found by the investigators in the drawer of the dresser, near the sink, at the far end of the kitchen, 8 feet from the bed? No one completely tidied up or washed the dishes that night, as we can see from the photograph, although Mrs Johnston could have put some things away before she left. Theoretically, Queen could have put it out of Chrissie's temptation, fearing that she might cut her throat, especially since it had been brought to her attention.

It is obvious that Chrissie would not have placed the knife in the drawer after using it to cut the rope in preparation for a terrifying deed. It should have been lying on the floor, the bed, a chair, the table... The problem, however, with this kind of thinking is, as we have said, that we do not know if Queen tampered with the scene for whatever possibly muddled motivation. Nor is it certain that the bread knife was the relevant implement; it nowhere appears, for instance, that cord fibres were found on or near it, or that the saw-teeth matched the cuts. Only half seriously, Sir Sidney Smith wondered if, goaded beyond endurance, Queen had cut the cord and thrown it to Chrissie as a challenge to do what she was threatening. That explanation could, indeed, account for his perplexity of mind and fear that he might be blamed.

The jury convicted by a majority of ten to five. The minority were all for Not Proven, none for Not Guilty. An appeal failed, but the capital sentence was respited. He was released years later, and worked again as a bookmaker's clerk in Glasgow, dying in May, 1958. He was said to have made friends and become well-liked in his circle, with his past not known.

Does this pattern of behaviour suggest a strong degree of fortitude and determination to make the best of his left-over life, or was he perhaps, in complete denial?

CHAPTER 3
THE HALF-MUTCHKIN

It was Saturday night in Edinburgh, and the party of young men swaying along Broughton Street in search of livelier entertainment had dined all too well. There were six of them, in variant degree intoxicated, and they came from respectable backgrounds. William Howat, soon to be no more, was clerk to Thomas Johnston, writer, (i.e. solicitor) and he shared lodgings at a house in Broughton Street with Henry Kerr, a land-surveyor.

That evening of February 8th, 1823, the two friends had put on a dinner party for four of their circle of acquaintances: Walter Grieve, a medical student, Alexander Welsh, a cattle-dealer at Balerno, James Johnston, whose occupation was not revealed, and John Wilkinson, who kept an inn at Bristo Street. Kerr was their spokesman, a man of the world: Johnston was an innocent and a spoilsport.

They sat down at the table at 5.00pm and rose at 9.00pm when the night was still young and tempting. Between them, they had consumed at least two and a half bottles of spirits, probably four, (naturally, accounts varied) and whisky toddy was downed after dinner as the next stage of the party was discussed. The initial plan was to walk Welsh and Johnston home to their lodgings at Wilkinson's establishment. They set off. Howat was 'rather drunk, but walked well' and spoke 'rather correctly'. Kerr is describing their progress. He himself was very little affected, but he would say that, wouldn't he? Johnston and Welsh were sober (a dubious proposition, in the light of later events) and Wilkinson, who had joined the dinner party halfway through, 'was not very much intoxicated and walked without any assistance' – a clear euphemism! In fact, he admitted afterwards that he had been 'a good deal intoxicated'.

Someone of the company suggested that they should all go to Cooper's Brittania tavern, but Johnston objected that Cooper was a boxer. Irritated by his squeamishness, the others decided to play a joke on him, and heartily recommended Anderson's house on the east side of the South Bridge as a jolly good tavern. It was, in reality, a house of ill repute, but it turned out that all the apartments were occupied, and they could not gain admittance. Directly across the street at 82 South Bridge was Mrs Mary McKinnon's similar establishment. Henry Kerr had been there before, in 1817. Madame was out visiting, but some girls opened the door willingly enough and the tipsy, noisy party streamed into the dark, candle-lit rooms, rather overwhelming, swamping, the outnumbered occupants, all female. The attendant harpies were Mary Curly, Elizabeth MacDonald, a stout woman of uncertain temper, and Elizabeth Gray.

At first the mood was merry. A half-mutchkin of spirits (equal to half a pint) was ordered, and two shillings was paid out for it. The girls drank with them, and hoped for more. There was a bed in the room, and a sofa, and one of the men lay down on the bed. There was a spot of dalliance – Welsh saw Wilkinson with his hand around Elizabeth MacDonald – but I do not think that anything orgiastic was in view. Although some of the men were obviously comfortable in a brothel, this was just a kind of communal, naughty spree and they were quite drunk. Besides, wet blanket Johnston was still there, nurturing suspicions of the kind of house they had entered, but not seeming more anxious than the others to leave it.

After perhaps half an hour, it was time to go home, but the young gentlemen had not lived up to their promise and their entertainment had not been sufficiently remunerative. They were pressed to take a further half-mutchkin each. Elizabeth MacDonald was the most vociferous in resenting their leaving the premises and she 'opposed their going'. Gradually, things were starting to get nasty. Walter Grieve saw Kerr lift up a chair and slam it down. The tinder had been lit. Elizabeth MacDonald pressed for payment, claiming, wrongly, that the chair was broken.

Welsh, Wilkinson and Johnston decided on a quick exit and were lucky to get out of the house when a servant opened the outside door for them. For a moment, we shall leave them there, going up the steps to the street. Meanwhile, Henry Kerr left the room with the bed and the sofa and made his way to the kitchen, trying to get out of the house and arguing with the strumpets. Elizabeth Gray gave his coat a slight pull, in the passage. Howat came, too. There were some women in the kitchen whom Kerr had not seen before, especially two crones, who appeared to be servants to the curious ménage. The kitchen door was then locked on them, but only temporarily. As he persisted in trying to escape, Elizabeth MacDonald seized Kerr with both hands and tore the frill of his shirt and his vest. She tripped him and he landed on all fours on the ground. His hat flew off. When he struggled to his feet, she grabbed him again, like a she-cat, angry and swearing. He took hold of her gown and tripped *her*. She fell, but he had not thrown her down. The door was opened. Round about now, Walter Grieve, the medical student, looked into the kitchen and saw William Howat strike Elizabeth MacDonald on the head. Both Kerr and Grieve were aware that the solicitor's clerk was seriously intoxicated.

Kerr went out into the passage and Grieve said, 'Don't strike a woman.' 'Certainly not,' he replied with drunken dignity. She was still provoking him. Wilkinson and Welsh had appeared in the passage, having returned to help their friends when they heard a disturbance, women's cries and a 'quarrelling with tongues'. Johnston, who had had more than enough of the discreditable night out, had decamped. Five men were now at loose in the dark, unfamiliar, hostile house. Shapes of people were going back and forth along the passage.

Seeing a new quarry, Elizabeth MacDonald flew at Wilkinson with clenched fists and struck him a blow on the chest. 'You b****!' he said. 'Why do you strike me?' He was furious, and Welsh held his hands to stop him from hitting her. The light in the passage went out as a result of the commotion. Kerr returned to the kitchen to extricate Howat. At some stage, Alexander Welsh heard Elizabeth MacDonald scream out. He thought this was when Howat hit her on the head, but Kerr was quite clear that Welsh and Wilkinson had not yet come back from the street. Could this have been another assault on the aggressive woman? She now had another go at Kerr. Grieve saw her take up a candlestick, as if to use it, and he took it away from her.

As the fracas had worsened, Mary Curly had run to fetch her mistress, Mary McKinnon, who was hob-nobbing with her crony, Samuel Hodge, a grocer, at his house in the Cowgate. June Lundie, of Leith Walk, was also a guest. This new group moved fast to 82 South Bridge. Madame went in like a fury and stormed along the passage to the kitchen, which had become the centre of the storm. 'Stand back, let me get a knife, and I'll let you see me settle the ****!' she shouted. Then she went deliberately to the dresser-table at the back of the door, put both hands into the knife-box and there was a rattling noise as if she were making a selection. Kerr's next glimpse of her was as she loomed in a dark corner with a table knife in her hand. It was some nine or ten inches long, sharpened to a point, with a black handle. She sprang at Kerr, but he parried her blow with his arm. Several of the women restrained her. Kerr told her that he would have thought she had more sense. She did not recognize him from his previous visit, and said nothing. He spoke to his friends in the passage – Welsh was restraining Wilkinson. Then he saw Howat keeping the women at bay.

There were no cries: it was quiet. As Kerr saw it happen, Mary McKinnon aimed a blow at Howat with her right hand, which she raised above her shoulder, making a sweep until the blade reached his left side. It was a 'back blow' with the point of the knife turned downwards.

Kerr seized her by the back of the neck and tripped her up, that being, apparently, his favourite manoeuvre when dealing with unpeaceable women. Turning to his friend, he found a scratch below his right eye, and blood flowing from his left side. Kerr placed him on a chair, and he breathed, 'Henry, she has given me enough,' before losing consciousness. The focus now shifts. Objective outsiders, professional people there to help and investigate, dispel the fumes of alcohol and mindless aggression. The bemused figures blundering around in the semi-darkness are sobering up and realizing that something terrible has happened.

The police were called. James Stuart, apprentice to Mr Law, surgeon, arrived at the same time. An agitated Mary McKinnon met him and told him that some people had come into the house and knocked down several of the inmates. He found Howat seated on a chair in a corner of the kitchen: his breathing was impeded and he was in a state of stupor. On examination, there was a large wound in the chest. Mr Black, police surgeon, also attended and Howat was conveyed to the Royal Infirmary. The police, bombarded with discrepant accounts, removed all parties to the police office for statements to be taken. The brothel-house keeper was detained. She claimed that Wilkinson had stabbed Howat. William Howat lingered until February 20th, having emitted a dying declaration and after he had identified Mary McKinnon as his attacker: she was brought to his death-bed.

And so the trial of Mary McKinnon on the charge of murder began on March 14th, 1823, before the High Court of Justiciary at Edinburgh. She pleaded Not Guilty and was prepared for a fierce fight for her life, represented at some expense by the impressive legal team of Francis Jeffrey and Henry Cockburn. The prisoner in the dock did not present the appearance of a typical harridan, being aged only about 30 and having a fallen air about her. Her counsel were to bring Captain Brown, formerly Superintendent of Police, to attest to her superior background. Her father had been quartermaster in the same regiment as that in which he had been adjutant, and he had known her from her 15th year. He had always considered her as inclining towards a humane disposition. She had been debauched by an officer, and afterwards shamefully neglected by her parents, to which he attributed her subsequent way of life. He had never considered her house as more disorderly than others of the same sort. (A desperate point.)

Her written statements were put in and read, to the effect that she had kept a 'licensed tavern' for several years: on the night in question, she was sent for because a party had entered her house in a state of intoxication. She had found a riot, with cries of murder; acts of violence were committed, furniture destroyed and she herself knocked down. If the deceased had received any blow in the scuffle which ensued, it was in circumstances which must free her from guilt.

James Johnston, who had made an excuse and left, was lucky not to be called by the Crown, but the other four survivors were there, disgraced in Edinburgh, revealed as players in a fatal brawl. Their own and joint endeavour was to minimise their drunkenness and to reduce the violence offered by them to the unruly women. Mary McKinnon's staff were loyal to her to the point of blatant perjury. Elizabeth MacDonald so incensed the Lord Justice Clerk with her contradictions that he said that he would feel it his duty to tell the jury that they ought not to give the slightest credit to her! After she had been cautioned, the second half of her evidence was taken down in writing, and perhaps she was then a little more careful.

No one believed the stout one, but what she said was that Wilkinson and the dead man were much intoxicated and the others hearty. She and Wilkinson quarrelled, because Wilkinson had been taking improper liberties with her. He struck her in the passage and struck her in the kitchen. Kerr came into the kitchen and hit her on the breast with a candlestick, making it black and blue. (There obviously was a candlestick on the scene.) A short time later, he punched her in the face and made her bleed. One of the old women, Margaret McInnes, took the candlestick from him as she was washing her face. Unfortunately, the bloodied face came after the candlestick attack, and here she prevaricated and became muddled and reprimanded by the Court. Coaxed by Jeffrey, who was permitted to examine her in the interests of truth, she expressed herself as now uncertain about the timing of the incident, an important one, as we shall see.

Chastened, perhaps, Elizabeth MacDonald continued: the door was not locked and the men could have left at any time. The disturbance was so serious that she sent Mary Curly for the prisoner, who might be a protection to them. Her mistress had no sooner come into the kitchen than she was knocked down by Wilkinson, who tore her cap: 'Murder!' she cried, but got up again. Wilkinson attacked her again in the passage, holding her by the wrist, and she begged the police, who had by then arrived, to take that man away from her, because he was breaking her arm. After this, Elizabeth MacDonald saw Howat sitting in the kitchen, and thought he was asleep; the last time she had seen him was when he was lying on the bed in the room in which they had been drinking, apparently intoxicated.

Elizabeth Gray, a young girl, was not caught in any inconsistencies. One of the party threw himself on a bed, and the others called for toddy. One 'used improper freedom' with Elizabeth MacDonald, who called them something on the lines of a 'parcel of low fellows'. (Her objections seem out of place, since she was chief prostitute in a brothel, but no doubt the lesser money offered for the wrong services was at the root of some of the trouble.) She, Elizabeth Gray, saw Elizabeth MacDonald lying on the kitchen floor at the beginning of the row. One of the men (she was totally unable to distinguish the revellers) hit *her* on the back of the neck, and she fell in the passage. Later, she saw her mistress, whom she had seen going into the kitchen, out in the passage with her cap off and her hair hanging about her neck.

Old Margaret McInnes said that her mistress was knocked down as soon as she went into the kitchen. She herself had been struck by some of the men and they had put her out into the passage.

Mr Black, the police surgeon at the scene, was the first witness for the defence, and his observations were very important, even if they did not receive much attention in court. He attended stout Elizabeth MacDonald at 82 South Bridge several days after the incident. She was in bed and said that she had received a blow on her left breast, apparently from a fist. (Not a candlestick.) When she had been brought to the police office on the night of the 8th, she had marks on her face from blows.

The surgeon had also attended the prisoner for some days after her arrest. She had seemed much troubled in body and mind, complaining that her head was hurt, and she showed him a mark on her side which she attributed to the disturbance at her house. Although he never saw any such symptoms, she also claimed to have a 'spitting of blood'. James Christie, turnkey in the lock-up-house, did see her spit blood five or six mornings after she came there. It was only after she washed herself.

John Smith, a boy about 15 years of age, had some new evidence not corroborated by the other defence witnesses. He knew the prisoner and he was in Hodge the grocer's house when a girl named Curly came in and said that some men were going to put Elizabeth MacDonald on the fire. He ran ahead of Mary McKinnon and when he got to the house, some of the men were preparing to put Elizabeth on the fire, but she resisted. The prisoner sent him for the watchmen; he found them at the head of Blair Street and brought them down. (Before going to Hodge's, he had been sent on an errand to the Abbey, so he, too, was on Mary McKinnon's staff.)

Closing for the Crown, the Solicitor General set the moral tone of the forum. Captain Brown's testimony had rendered the case even more painful and melancholy, and he would not judge harshly those vices which arose from degradation. There were passions which his sex had contributed to form. Marked depravity was exhibited by the witnesses on both sides, and they had committed wilful and horrible perjury. He referred to self-defence or provocation but was himself satisfied that there was no justification for the use of a lethal weapon.

And indeed the Lord Justice Clerk strongly favoured Kerr's evidence and ruled that, in point of law, there was nothing before the court that would support self-defence or provocation. It was interesting, however, that the jury, convicting by a majority, begged leave to recommend mercy, again by a majority. The Court could not discern any grounds whatsoever for such a recommendation. Dire and thunderous were the final improving homiletic words from the Bench and the poor creature in her black figured sarsnet gown, black bonnet and veil, swooned and shrieked and groaned.

The trial of the brothel-house keeper had been greatly enjoyed by the populace and 20,000 excited persons attended the execution at the head of Libberton's Wynd on April 16th, the body afterwards delivered over to Dr Monro, Professor of Anatomy, for public dissection. Lord Henry Cockburn, distinguished Scottish judge, kept a remarkably frank diary, and in *Circuit Journeys* (published posthumously in 1888) recorded that Mary McKinnon died 'gracefully and bravely;

and her last moment was marked by a proceeding so singular, that it is on its account that I mention her case. She had an early attachment to an English Jew, who looked like a gentleman, on the outside at least; and this passion had never been extinguished. She asked him to come and see her before her fatal day. He did so; and on parting, finally, on her last evening, she cut an orange into two, and giving him one half, and keeping the other herself, directed him to go to some window opposite the scaffold, at which she could see him, and to apply his half to his lips when she applied her half to hers. All this was done; she saw her only earthly friend, and making the sign, died cheered by this affection.'

Less romantically, however, Cockburn goes on to say that, 'She had left everything she had, amounting to £4,000 or £5,000, to her friend. He took the legacy, *but refused to pay the costs of her defence*, which her agent only screwed out of him by an action.'

For our purposes now, the most telling, if tantalizing, part of Lord Cockburn's account is his view that 'If some circumstances which were established in a precognition, taken by the orders of Sir Robert Peel, then Home Secretary, after her conviction, had transpired on the trial, it is more than probable that Jeffrey, whose beautiful speech, on the bad elements in his hands, is remembered to this hour, would have prevailed on the jury to restrict their conviction to culpable homicide.'

The reference to culpable homicide indicates that Cockburn had provocation not self-defence, in mind, since a successful plea of self-defence exonerates the defendant outright. However, Walter Grieve, the medical student, braver than his friends, did say that he saw the deceased strike Elizabeth MacDonald on the head. Moreover, there was medical evidence of an assault on her. Mary McKinnon surely knew by the time that she picked up the knife that her henchwoman had received the injury most feared by all women, whatever the century, a hard blow on the breast. A person may kill to prevent the murder of another. She was placed in a defensive position, fearing she knew not what future violence.

The three minutes' lapse of time – if Kerr was correct – between taking up the knife and delivering the fatal blow, to which one might add the deliberate selection of the sharpened knife, went strongly against a plea of provocation. Who knows what really happened in the dark kitchen? A legal definition of provocation (Lord Jamieson in 1938) seems to represent Mary McKinnon's position: 'Being agitated and excited, and alarmed by violence, I lost control over myself, and took life, when my presence of mind had left me, and with no thought of what I was doing.'

We shall never know what atrocious behaviour, previously concealed, had come to light. Who was the new informant with the conscience? It had to be someone who was in the kitchen or could see into the room, at the relevant time. That lets Johnston out. Otherwise, he would have been a promising candidate. Was it an aged crone? Or was it one of the young gentlemen, letting the side down?

CHAPTER 4
TO THE
LIGHTHOUSE

If someone cursed with second sight had told Lord Cockburn then that a particularly callous murder would be committed over a century later at the picturesque site which he was visiting, I doubt if he would have turned a hair. As a famous circuit judge, regularly trying capital murders, he had few illusions about man's inhumanity to man, and found solace in nature and beauty.

On September 26th, 1844, he had gone to the lighthouse... 'Yesterday was given to an expedition to the lighthouse on the island of Little Ross, about six or seven miles below Kirkcudbright. Some rode and some drove ... till we all came to the alehouse on the peninsula of Great Ross, where we took boat, and after about a mile's sailing, were landed on the island. It is one of the lesser lights. All its machinery was explained to us by a sensible keeper. I never understood the thing before. The prospect from the top, and, indeed, from every part of the island, is beautiful. But I was more interested in the substantial security and comfort of the whole buildings, both for scientific and for domestic purposes. No Dutchman's summerhouse could be tidier. Everything, from the brass and the lenses of the light to the kitchen, and even to the coalhouse, of each of the two keepers, was as bright as a jeweller's shop.'

Quite so: a lighthouse is a potent symbol of order in chaos, where harmony and reason prevail. Inside the tower of light there should be a safe stillness. It was unheard of for keeper to turn on keeper, as sadly happened here in 1960. An unsuitable individual had, somehow, slipped through the net. It was not even a specially isolated posting. One keeper's wife lived in on the island, and they kept chickens. The victim thought the world of his keeper-killer and suspected no evil to the end.

The murder was discovered earlier than the killer would have expected, as if there were some measure of retribution, and he was soon captured. Thomas Robertson Collin, a bank manager of Strathdee, Kirkcudbright, was the involuntary *deus ex machina*. Thursday, August 18th, was a local holiday, and he and his 19-year-old son, an architecture student, decided to go sailing in the bay, which widens out to the Irish Sea, with the rushing Solway Firth to the east, and a rocky coast riddled with smugglers' caves. It was not a pleasant place to be at the mercy of the elements, and when the weather deteriorated after an hour or so's sailing, at 12.30pm, they thought it safer to put in at Little Ross Island, which stands at the mouth of the bay, and wait for the next tide. Lord Cockburn's descriptive powers show the significance of the Kirkcudbright tide, which 'rises at an average about 20 or 25 feet, and often a great deal more – sometimes 35. This great flow fills up all the bays, making a brim-full sea for three miles above the town, and for six or eight below it. It is then a world of waters.'

Harmless trespassers, seeking respite as they were, the Collin pair felt obliged to state their business, but there was no sign of life at the lighthouse and the two keepers' cottages. Apparently the lighthouse was not continuously manned during the hours of daylight, because Collin assumed, at first, that one man was out fishing, and the other sleeping. A telephone rang from time to time. At 4 o'clock, on the brink of leaving with the tide, feeling slightly uneasy, he made one last reconnoitre, and boldly looked through a rear window. A still, human form was lying on a bed, under the bedclothes, with just the head showing.

Collin ran round to the front of the cottage and entered. 'What's the matter?' he called out, but there was no reply. He approached the body of the man and found no pulse and the hand cold. He removed the towel which was draped over the head, and underneath it there was a great deal of blood. Three pieces of rope lay on the bed, there was more on the floor, and a pool of blood. Outside, he told his son to try to get the attention of one of the fishing boats which were bobbing in the bay, and then he used the telephone in the lighthouse to call the police and a doctor.

Robert Milligan, a Kirkcudbright fisherman, was out that day, and he spotted young Collin waving frantically from the rocks. He came ashore, and soon identified the dead man as Hugh Clark, aged 62, relief lighthouse keeper, a native of Dalry, Castle Douglas. A World War I veteran, he had been a postman for 40 years. The three living men standing on that island searched in fear for the other keeper who should have been there – Robert McKenna Cribbes Dickson, a young man, 24, who was in charge of the lighthouse while the principal keeper, John Thomson, was away on holiday with his wife. Collin's son examined the lighthouse logbook, and found that the last entry had been made at 3.00am on the previous morning. There was a .22 rifle lying against a wall in a storeroom, but it turned out to be unconnected with events.

The situation was beginning to feel like the great mystery of the Eilean Mor lighthouse, located in a much more lonely environment right out in the Atlantic Ocean, 25 kilometres west of the Hebridean island of Lewis. Lashed by gales on the most northern of the seven Flannan Isles, known as the Seven Hunters, Lord Cockburn would have found this a major light! It was completed in 1899. On Boxing Day, 1900, the tender *Hesperus* landed a relief keeper, together with stores and belated Christmas presents. She was a week late, after heavy storms. Normally she came every six weeks.

Here, too, as at Little Ross, there was no sign of life. Three keepers had vanished from the face of the rock. Their boat was still in its cradle. Two sets of oilskins and sea boots were missing, but the third was intact. The last entry in the log was dated December 15th. There had been a fierce, destructive gale. Later, too late, it was discovered that a freak wave would occasionally wash over the west landing.

A fisherman's launch, quickly scrambled, now brought to Little Ross two police officers and a doctor. When Dr Rutherford turned the body over to examine the back of the head, a bullet fell out of the left eye socket. There were a couple of bullet holes in the bedhead. It was not a case of suicide, with three head wounds, decidedly not self-inflicted. Clark appeared to have been shot while asleep. His legs were sticking out of the bed in an odd way, but the doctor thought that this was the result of a reflex action. Death had occurred about 10 hours before the body was discovered.

Glasgow detectives, called in to assist, estimated that bullets had been fired from a shortened rifle, because the direction of the shots was from the narrow space at the window side of the bed where there was very little room to move. The angle was tight. The ropes seemed to be part of an abandoned plan.

The theory that Dickson, too, had been murdered by a third party who had then vanished from the island, spiriting away the second corpse, never got off the ground, although, at that stage, nothing to Dickson's detriment was current. John Thomson, the principal keeper, considered him to be a good, responsible employee, on cordial terms with the murdered man. Mrs Thomson had noticed that he did not talk much, but he often had coffee with them, and he was 'very helpful with feeding the chickens'. Thomson interrupted his holiday to return to the lighthouse and found that his .22 rifle was missing, and about £30 had been taken from his cash-box, on which, in due course, Dickson's fingerprints were verified.

Dickson as he fled had left a trail of hot clues. Dr

Rutherford had placed the murder at about 6 o'clock in the early hours of Thursday, August 18th. The young man had then rowed off in Hugh Clark's dinghy, which was found 'tied up perpendicularly' on rocks at Manor Hole in Ross Bay on the mainland. Its precarious position showed that it had been beached at high tide, which was given as between 4.00 and 6.00am. In fact, the plane of the boat was so steep that the outboard motor touched the rocks below.

Moving on to Ross Farm, where Hugh Clark had kept his old 10hp Wolseley car when he was on duty, Dickson drove off in the vehicle without being heard. Mrs Catherine Leslie, who lived at the farm with her son, seeing the car gone, knew that Clark had not taken it, because two ancient overcoats which he used to cover the tyres to protect them from the sun, were strewn across the road instead of being neatly folded on the grass at the side. Robert Maxwell, a dairyman employed at Ross Dairy actually saw Dickson drive past in Hugh Clark's car at 9.10 on the Thursday morning. This seems rather late. The distances were not great. Had he been sitting and thinking somewhere, stunned?

Worse, he had then crashed the old grey car, colliding with a van in Maxwelltown, and had given the van driver his real name on a scrap of paper – 'R. Dickson. Ross Lighthouse'. The following afternoon, the Wolseley was found abandoned in Summerville Road, Dumfries. Before 9.10 on the Thursday, however, Dickson had engaged in some proactive doings; he had telephoned a car-hire company in Dumfries, giving his name as Thomson, and arranged to hire a car for two days. Later that morning, he turned up and collected a Hillman Husky, producing a driving licence in the name of John Thomson. He seemed to have a great deal of cash in hand as he paid out the requisite £7. Off he drove, many miles south-east across the Pennines as far as Selby, in the West Riding of Yorkshire. Perhaps he was making for the coast and a passage abroad.

What he had not allowed for was the unscheduled arrival

of the bank manager on the island. It emerged that mail and supplies were delivered to Little Ross every Wednesday. George Poland, a fisherman of Kirkcudbright, had performed that service for the Lighthouse Commissioners for 20 years, and on the day before the murder, on his regular visit, he had handed two registered letters to Dickson, who, we may remember, was keeper in charge for the time being. One envelope contained Hugh Clark's wages, the other, money for paying the tradesmen. Dickson had opened the first envelope and handed Clark his cash. The older man had put it in his pocket. Theoretically, then (and the attack could have been deliberately timed for an early Thursday morning) Dickson had a whole week in which to escape before George Poland came again. The reality, however, must have been that it would soon have been noticed that the lighthouse was unmanned, and we have the detail that the telephone was ringing and not being answered. How often did those 'tradesmen' call from Kirkcudbright, anyway?

The description of the hired car and the missing man was circulated nation-wide. At 8.15am on Friday the 19th, two constables on duty in Yorkshire stopped the Hillman Husky. PC John Lister opened the car door and took hold of the driver's hands. He seemed very surprised to be apprehended, but freely admitted that he was Robert Dickson. When cautioned, he said, 'All right, I know all about it.' There was a loaded rifle between the front seats. The barrel had been shortened and the wooden butt had been sawn off just behind the trigger. They found a quantity of ammunition in the car and there was over £80 in cash in Dickson's pockets, together with John Thomson's driving licence. The principal keeper identified the rifle as his .22, and said that it had been sawn into three pieces. The sawn-off butt of a rifle was discovered in a cupboard in the lighthouse workshop.

On November 27th, 1960, Robert McKenna Cribbes Dickson was brought up at the High Court in Dumfries before

Lord Cameron, charged on indictment with capital murder and thefts of (*inter alia*) the victim's car, boat and wages. He pleaded Not Guilty. Chief Detective Inspector Thomas Joyce of the Glasgow CID, who had led the investigation, stated that Dickson held a Royal Navy educational test certificate, but his service was described on discharge as 'fair'. His background was beginning to become clear. The defence brought extensive psychiatric evidence. Dr Andrew Wyllie, superintendent of Aberdeen Royal Mental Hospital, testified that he had first seen Dickson in 1957 after he had taken an overdose of aspirins on his way back to the navy after being absent without leave. He gave a history of falling from a horse followed by severe headaches. There had been tears as he recounted his history, admitting to a period in an approved school and theft of a car, and as he spoke he went through the motions of smoking without a cigarette. His diagnosis had been that of psychopathic personality and he had been treated as a voluntary patient at the hospital. Dr Wyllie now described him as 'episodically on the borderline of insanity with reactions which were abnormal under conditions of stress'.

Dr John Cochrane, a prison doctor, had found Dickson coldly indifferent and unaffected by his situation even when confronted by the gravity of the crime charged and the possible penalty. The superintendent of Glasgow Royal Mental Hospital, Dr Angus McIven, who had also been asked to have a look at the prisoner, similarly inclined to the diagnosis of psychopathy bordering on insanity. (CDI Joyce had found Dickson quite lucid and intelligent with nothing abnormal in his behaviour, but he did notice that his general conversation was about motor cars – not, one would have thought, an appropriate topic for someone in his predicament.)

Lord Cameron bent over backwards to ensure that the defendant's mental state was fully ventilated, himself asking the principal keeper, 'Was there any sign of his being a brooding type of man or a melancholy one?... Was he in any way irrational or did he appear to act abnormally in any way?' The answer to both questions was in the negative. Dr Edgar Rintoul, who had conducted the post-mortem, testified that the bullets had been fired from a range of about six inches; there were two major injuries, and a suicide would have been incapable of inflicting the second one. The deceased had offered no resistance, which ruled out accident during a struggle.

The Advocate-Depute, in his closing speech, referred to the shooting as a cold, calculated, deliberate, brutal, black-hearted murder, which took the jury back hundreds of years to the type of crime that was committed when people were far less civilised. In his summing up, Lord Cameron contributed to the case the memorable phrase that Dickson had left his trail 'blazing round the Stewartry of Kirkcudbright'.

The jury speedily returned a majority verdict of Guilty and Dickson was sentenced to be hanged at Saughton Prison, Edinburgh, on December 21st. However, more than a hint of psychopathy had been uncovered, with a possibility of brain damage and he was reprieved five days before the date of execution, to serve life imprisonment. It is wrong to presume that psychopaths are too cold and remote to experience depression. They are, in fact just as likely as any other to commit suicide, upset by the consequences of their aberrant actions, or oppressed by the bleakness of being themselves. Dickson had already evinced a suicidal proclivity when stressed, and, two years into his sentence, he was found dead from a overdose of drugs in his cell at Peterhead Prison.

CHAPTER 5
MR KELLO'S
SUNDAY MORNING
SERVICE

The minister was on form that Sunday morning, when he preached a fiery moving sermon. The turning pebbles of his oratory fell in a silver shower on the bowed heads of his congregation. Mr Kello was transported, his face working with the ripples of the divine afflatus. Poor Mrs Kello was not in her pew, but that was only to be expected, because she had been ailing for some weeks. The minister had confided to certain people, in hushed tones, that his wife had been tempted to put an end to herself. Sick she had been, on and off, and he, too, lately.

The homily over, the plain little kirk emptied and the parishioners went home to their dinner. Spott was just a speck of a village, its name meaning, indeed, a small spot of ground. Set between Dunbar and the sea, three miles to the north, and the rising, red-soiled Lammermuirs, with its own mound, Brant Hill, it had a dark history. In October, 1705, the Kirk Session minutes recorded, 'Many witches burnt on the top of Spott Loan' and that is where the last wailing witch in the whole of Scotland was done to death.

Witchcraft was in the very air, and the absolute belief that the Evil One stalked the land froze the blood with fear of shadows. There is no evidence, only rumour, that John Kello was connected with witchcraft, or that he was a taker of witches. He himself was to swear that he had not been initiated in 'wicked practises of the Magicienis' and had no desire to probe beyond the given Word of God. If you can find a dusty old copy, there is in existence a fine, scary novel, *Mr Kello*, by John Ferguson (Harrap, 1924) which is based on the premise that he was entirely consumed by the occupation of not suffering a witch to live: 'He lived behind a barred door in the dark, mournful study, where he wrote by sunlight and candlelight year after year upon *The Discoverie of Satan – The Signs by which a Witch may be Condemned'*.

What really interested the minister of Spott, however, was his own temporal station in life. Edinburgh would have been more to his taste. A man of the people who had studied hard, an ornament of the reformed Kirk of Scotland, he felt that he was kept down and not receiving adequate respect or recompense. With a little money in hand, he began to dabble in investment in property, enjoying the 'filthie ocker' (interest), but his luck ran out and his affairs became complicated. He fretted and brooded.

Meanwhile, the parish was glad to be served by the Reverend John Kello, who had bettered himself, a scholar to be sure, and a fine preacher, with an impeccable wife, Margaret (Thomson), also of humble origins, and their three children, Bartilmo, Barbara and Bessie. Alas! The family picture lied; Margaret blocked the minister's ladder, and he had set his sights on the laird's daughter. Secret like a worm in the recesses of his perfidious heart was the hope that he might succeed in marrying a real lady.

Margaret had to die. He laid out rumours of her indisposition and her melancholy, like a scent, let it be known that he had made a will in her favour, as if he had a presentiment that he would predecease her, and watched for an opportunity. Forty days passed, during which the Enemy did not cease from tempting him, and after this significant period, he developed a mysterious illness which, with hindsight, he perceived as a sign from God. Pretending, however, that Margaret was similarly afflicted, he tried to poison her, but her constitution was so strong that she merely voided the substance.

That Sunday of the resounding sermon, September 24th, 1570, afterwards, he asked some neighbours to come back to the manse with him, to cheer up Mrs Kello. She would appreciate the company. He accompanied them across the kirkyard to his front door, but found it locked from the inside. He appeared puzzled and concerned. There was another entrance, seldom used, which opened into his study, and he left the others to wait outside (just as William Herbert Wallace, five centuries later, caused his neighbours, witnesses, to wait while he went in to see if his wife, Julia, was all right).

Soon they heard his ululations of woe, and, venturing, in, found their minister lamenting by the dangling, crook-necked figure of his wife, swaying on a rope suspended from a hook in the ceiling of her bedroom. The tableau of suicide spoke for itself, and sympathy washed over the widower and his motherless bairns. The real story was that John Kello had strangled Margaret Kello with a towel as she knelt at her devotions. 'In the verie death,' he confessed, 'she could not beleive I bure hir ony evill will, bot was glaid, as sche than said, to depairt, gif her death could doe me ather vantage or pleasoure.'

The Reverend Andrew Simpson, of Dunbar, had visited John Kello on his sickbed while his wife yet lived, and Kello had imparted to him a dramatic vision, or dream, or even hallucination, which he had experienced, and when, now Kello went to him for comfort in his role of grieving, bewildered widower, Simpson suddenly became seized with a prophetic force. It was a great moment in the history of crime. He rose to his feet and addressed the shivering sinner:

'Brother,' he said, 'I doe remember quhan I visitate yow, in tyme of your grit seiknes, ye did open to me that visione; that ye war caried be ane grym man befoir the face of ane

terrible Judge, and to escaip his furie ye did precipitate your
self in ane deip river, when his angelis and messingeris did
follow you with two-edged swords; and ever quhan thai struike
at you, ye did declyne and jowke [dodge] in the water; while
in the end, by ane way unknowin to you, ye did escape.'

Sigmud Freud himself could have done no better as the
Reverend Simpson launched into his analysis: John Kello was
the author of the cruel murder then conserved in his heart,
and he was carried before the terrible judgement seat of God
in his own conscience. The messenger of God was the law of
the land, before which he would be judged. The water in
which he stood was his own vain hypocrisy.

Mr Simpson of Dunbar achieved some popular acclaim for
this feat of interpretation, but when, seven years later, he
foretold the loss of the local fishing fleet wrecked off Dunbar,
unfairly, he was more blamed than approbated. John Kello,
his secret disclosed, withdrew to consider his options. He
could flee abroad or stay and face the music. If he repented
privately, would that do? Mr Simpson pressed him so hard
that in the end Kello believed that God spoke through him,
and he voluntarily made his way to Edinburgh and there
confessed his crime to the Bench and the Church. Condemned
to be hanged and his body to be cast on the fire and burnt to
ashes, he seems to have got off lightly, considering the
ingenuity of the times, unless his cloth or his contrition saved
him from worse penalty. Suspicion of witchcraft was
undoubtedly attached to his name and he might have expected
the flames on the hill.

At first, his whole property was forfeit to the Crown, but
by one of those rare ameliorations for which we anxiously scan
the pages of history, the three children were allowed an
inheritance. And so the minister of Spott was hanged in
Edinburgh on October 4th, 1570, for the 'crewell and odious
murthure' of his wife. How the mighty periods of his
repentance rolled from the scaffold as he delivered his last

homily, 'to the great gude example and comfort of all the behalders'! He also left a posthumous confession. John Kello really takes the biscuit. To come to the pulpit with red hands, his wife left hanging from a hook, and preach a Sunday sermon, is unparalleled in hypocrisy. But was it hypocrisy to blame the temptations of the Devil – 'Thir were the glistering promises whairwith Sathan, efter his accustomed maner, eludit my senses' – when all around him shared his structure of beliefs?

CHAPTER 6
THE WHITEINCH ATROCITIES

Sometimes a dreadful murder can illuminate the most unremarkable area and reveal the everyday lives of the hoardes of scurrying people, otherwise obscure, soon forgotten. The obvious example is Whitechapel at the time of Jack the Ripper. Such a place, although by no means a depraved slumland, was Whiteinch at the turn of the century. The name means 'White Island' and it is situated on the north bank of the Clyde, beyond Partick, some three and a half miles from the centre of Glasgow. It grew up around the great shipyards in the middle of the 19th century, after dredging of the area. Quite self-contained, Whiteinch had a distinctive identity of its own, and because of the employment created by shipbuilding, it was never a region of no hope.

The inhabitants were mostly workers and their families, living in specially built 'workers' cottages', and tenements. The whole district was informed with a spirit of self-improvement, with workers' education, a good library, a public school, and Victoria Park with its grotto – a grove of fossils found on site in the mudflats when the park was being laid out. Some villas housed the lower management and professional classes such as engineers. Trams ran and a steam passenger ferry plied between Whiteinch and Linthouse.

Here, at 1122 Dumbarton Road, at the foot of one of those classic, red sandstone tenements (now replaced by modern flats) lived 50-year-old Miss Lucy McArthur, who kept a small dairy, with the shop at the front, and the room which was her solitary home at the back. Providing a vital service to the neighbourhood, she had plenty of customers and the business was surprisingly prosperous. It was her mistake, in her innocence as a woman living alone and handling cash, to have made herself a target for evil by letting it be known that she had £500 to fall back on.

On November 8th, 1904, early morning, her young 'message girls', Jeanie and Sarah Platt, knocked as usual at her shop door in order to collect the milk to deliver to her customers. There was no reply and the door was locked, which immediately alarmed them, because she was well known for her punctuality – the sort of person you could set your clock by. The girls went round for help to Mrs Macdonald, a neighbour who lived in the same close. She knew how to use the washing-house key to open the door. They peered inside. It was a scene of spattered blood and scattered bottles. Jeanie, the older girl, was sent to Whiteinch Police Office to report that something was wrong at the dairy, and Detective Inspector Mackenzie walked back to the shop with her and entered cautiously. There were signs of a mortal struggle and the drawers of the counter were open and empty.

Behind the counter, in the corner by the window, lay the battered body of Miss McArthur, the skull very obviously fractured. The hands were tied with two pieces of old, plaited cord, and a red cotton handkerchief was tied around the neck. She had been dead for 'several hours'. The inspector then entered the living premises, using the separate door in the close, which is not recorded as having been locked (for surely Miss McArthur intended shortly to return there). As he went in, he heard a tinkle, and, looking down, found the bloodstained key of the shop, outside on the threshold. In this inner room there was no disorder, only a tableau of sparse daily life. The gas light was still ablaze and the kettle had boiled dry on the gas burner at the fireplace, which was also still alight. A bullock's head was in a pot on the fire.

Apparently Miss McArthur had been preparing the delicacy known as potted head, possibly for her customers.

The corpse was raised and placed on a stretcher, whereupon the broken handle of a small hatchet, bloodstained and with adherent human hair, was seen on the floor. The steel head of the hatchet, similarly stained, was lying on the top of a box nearby. It was a typical household axe of the type used for breaking coals or sticks, the wooden shaft about 12 inches long, and with a hammerhead as well as a blade. It turned out that Miss McArthur, who, after all, was not an old woman, had put her trust in a bank. There was no hoard under the bed. Her bank books were found in the shop, and they did indicate, however, that she must had had a considerable sum of cash lodged somewhere on the premises, which was now missing. Moreover, on the day before the murder was discovered, a substantial account had been paid out to her, and she had her rent money, too, in readiness. A couple of £1 notes were lying on the floor beside some articles of clothing, and £6 10s was undisturbed in a hatbox.

The precise purpose for which Miss McArthur had withdrawn a considerable sum from the bank can only be a matter for conjecture. She could already have spent it. The assassin might have had some special knowledge that she was in funds. Whether or not he had searched her private room is not disclosed. One would surmise that she would have concealed a significant amount of money in the private premises, as in the hatbox (if that actually was in her room). Or did she by double bluff work out that the shop would be safer? Why did he tie her up and then kill her? Death must have come to her for psychological reasons – panic, excitement, frustration ... Of course, she had seen him and could identify him. Perhaps, indeed, she knew him.

The likelihood is that he was a local man, since he knew the circumstances of his quarry, and since he must, like Jack the Ripper, have been covered in blood as he fled. He was helped by darkness. Miss McArthur had been engaged in a little speciality cooking by gaslight on the previous November evening, presumably before bedtime. Surely she would not in the normal course of events have opened up her premises in the middle of the night (unless she was forced into the dairy)? On the other hand, we know from Jack the Ripper researches that in poor areas people were coming and going all night long, back and forth to work, slaughtering horses, and doing a spot of cobbling in the back yard ...

The police offered a reward of £200, but the murder remains unsolved to this day.

Later, it was officially conjectured that the same hand could have struck down Miss Marion Gilchrist, aged 82, in that famous and considerably more upmarket case of December 21st 1908. The victim here lived alone except for a maid at 15 Queen's Terrace, 49 West Princes Street, Glasgow and her circumstances seemed to be known to her killer. It was no secret that there was a treasure trove of jewellery kept in the flat. Detective Trench was asked to investigate the possibility that Oscar Slater, convicted and released after 18 years, had been involved in the Dairy Murder, but he found that Slater had not been in Glasgow at the relevant time. Anyway, the police valued an impression of a hobnailed boot found at the scene in 1904, and Oscar Slater was an out-and-out dandy.

The Whiteinch tenements were under scrutiny again in the 1920s. A cruel and nasty murder took place, and although poverty, need, and greed were supposed to have been at the root of the crime, they scarcely seem sufficient explanation. Elizabeth Benjamin, whose life was to be cut short at the age of 14, lived with her family in Dumbarton Road, where her father ran a credit drapery business from their home. A photograph of the sad girl in her best clothes has survived: small, pinched face, worldly-wise; luxuriant hair crowned by a best quality, shiny bow; pale, cotton, long-sleeved dress, with a necklace (coral?), a round brooch at the neck and a narrow, plaited belt. She smiles, pluckily, but her brow is anxious.

The family was Jewish, and if the murder had not been so soon solved, a racial element might have been suspected. The contemporary newspapers made a point of mentioning that the girl was a 'Jewess'. During the October of 1921, her father was ill, and she took on responsibility for the shop. Her elder sister, Esther, and her grown-up brother, Maxwell, both worked the tenements on a daily basis. On Mondays, the shop was closed, and Elizabeth trudged off on her own with a heavy suitcase packed with goods to sell on the doorstep. She was also charged with collecting customers' instalments, so that she was steadily garnering small sums of cash. On October 31st, Elizabeth Benjamin did not go home. Her last known call was at 4.00pm.

At 11.00pm, her family went to the police and reported her missing. Eight hours passed. At 7.00am, on November 1st, a woman found a girl's body in the back green of a tenement at 67 George Street, and covered it with a cloth. A photograph taken on site shows the peculiar position of the corpse, lying right at the bottom of the court, parallel with the wall, and with the feet in long boots stretched out and awkwardly protruding a few inches through the side railings as if the distance had been misjudged. Detectives working with Professor John Glaister, and his son, found no signs of a struggle. The body had been brought to the stark place where it lay, because the ground underneath it was dry, while the clothing and area around it were damp. The wrists had been methodically tied after death, to fashion a kind of handle for transportation. There were several misleading head wounds, exposing the bone of the forehead, which had probably only stunned the girl. The actual cause of death was asphyxia, caused by a small pocket handkerchief, which had been tightly jammed down the throat. There was no indication of sexual assault – the girl was *virgo intacta* – although the skirt was pulled up around the waist, either in an attempt to suggest a sexual motive or as a result of sheer haste and panic in the hours of darkness.

The body was removed to the police office, where Maxwell identified his murdered sister. The killers – for there were two – were not at all difficult to trace. Faced, as ever, with the problem of the disposal of the body in a crowded district, they had resorted merely to removing it from their home and dumping it in the court of the tenement in which they lived, in the full knowledge that the police would be bound to question them. The detectives soon concentrated their enquiries on a young married couple, William and Helen Harkness, living at number 67 with their little boy. Dr Sutherland, police surgeon, found bloodstains on their stairs and doorstep. The husband's tool of his trade, a riveter's reamer, bore stains which turned out to be human blood, as did those on the couple's clothing and furniture. Seventy articles were taken to the forensic medicine department for examination.

The police discovered the victim's suitcase in a back court nearby. Her cash book was still inside it, and neatly showed that she had had £1 9s 8d in her possession. Maxwell said that when his sister had left home in the morning she had had £1 in silver. The women of Whiteinch had been paying over to her small sums ranging from 1s to 3s 6d.

William and Helen Harkness were arrested, and someone must have cared for their son. On January 30th, 1922, they were put on trial at the High Court of Justiciary, Glasgow. Although they had lived in low poverty, in spite of the husband's trade at the shipyards, they look a spick enough pair in the dock, as if they are off to the dancing, he with wavy hair, she with pert features under a narrow-brimmed hat. The reality was, however, that both drank too much and they were badly in debt. The principal witness for the Crown was William Harkness's own brother, John, who lived at Douglas

Street. He was 33, two years older than William. At first he, too, had been co-accused of the murder and kept in custody for three months with the charge hanging over him. His story was uncorroborated and defence counsel, naturally, made much of that. Moreover, he had not formerly been on good terms with the Harkness couple. But he had helped them to dispose of the body.

He stated that he had been at his mother-in-law's home in Dumbarton Road on October 31st, 1921, when Helen Harkness (the accused woman) had called to say that brother Willie wanted to see him. This surprised him, since he was not on speaking terms with William and Helen. She asked him to join her for a drink in a public house where both had two glasses of whisky and he also drank half a pint of beer. She said she was in trouble and he agreed to go round to number 67. He arrived there at 8.00pm. Helen implored him, 'Surely you will help us? He is your own brother, your own flesh and blood.'

Then it was that William admitted that he had struck a woman on the head. They had been desperate for money. After all the trouble, they only got a pound and a few shillings. Helen said it was a lousy pound, and she would rather have had the factoress (rent collector to the tenement) and then they would have got about £50. They asked John Harkness to help them carry the body down to the Clyde or the canal. William took his brother to the washhouse and unlocked the door. Their light was just one candle, and a 'bundle' could be seen in the gloom, lying on the floor by the boiler, with the legs in their long boots sticking out.

For some reason (by whose counsel?) there was a change of plan and the two men carried the body to the back court where it was found. William cleaned up the washhouse floor. John was asked to jump over the railings and dispose of another bundle in the ashpit of a nearby close: he chose number 69. Probably this was bloodstained clothing. The house was full of smoke. Helen had been burning something in a bucket. John put the fire out with water. For the first time he noticed that there was blood about the place. He opened the window to let the smoke out. During all this, William's little boy was lying in bed. They showed John 'the woman's' suitcase. William wanted to burn it, but John was against it. He was getting disgusted and said that he was going back to his mother-in-law's. They stowed the suitcase in a common jute bag and put it in a back court several closes away.

The following evening, John went back to his brother's house. William handed him a newspaper, and for the first time he learnt that the 'woman' was a girl of 14. 'I see that she was gagged,' he said. 'Yes,' said Helen, 'She was a strong little bugger. My legs are all black and blue where she kicked me.' She had bitten William's finger.

That was the brother's story, and the jury believed him. It was curious, perhaps, that no one had witnessed the suspicious activities and come forward to corroborate his account, but the reason might have lain in solidarity in the tenements. There was some trouble during the trial when the court adjourned for lunch, and John was assaulted in the tea-room. No witnesses were brought for the defence. Counsel for the wife said that there was no evidence that she had suggested the robbery, but there was no doubt that her husband had struck the girl. 'Once you strike a blow, you have to finish it,' he had told John Harkness. However, the expert evidence about the asphyxia was very telling: hard as the defence tried to show that the handkerchief was a gag, Professor Glaister decisively blocked suggestions that the girl in her struggle could have drawn it in accidentally. It was rolled up in a tight ball and jammed back in the throat.

Husband and wife were both convicted of murder. He held her hand and patted her on the back as she cried when they were sentenced to death. For some reason, although she had, according to the evidence of John Harkness, said some vixenish things, there was a unanimous recommendation of mercy for Helen Harkness, presumably because of her gender and the fact that she had a young child. She was reprieved on February 18th and spent 15 years in prison, before being released on March 3rd, 1937. William Harkness was executed on February 21st, 1922. When the appointed day dawned, he had to be woken by his warders. To the end, all his concern had been for his wife. As for his brother, he seems to have been a marked man: on New Year's Eve, 1926, he was assaulted in a Glasgow bar, and died from his injuries the next day.

CHAPTER 7
DEATH OF
A HERMIT

The urge to leave family and home, if there is one, and set off on the open road as a tramp can indicate mental illness. From time immemorial, society has fluctuated in its tolerance, sometimes blessing the humble vagrant on his way, and sometimes seeking to cage him. These days, of course, the situation is complicated by drug abuse. If the individual happens upon a makeshift shelter which no one else wants, bearing a resemblance to a home that appeals to him, he will stay there for years if left in peace, gradually transmogrified into a hermit, growing increasingly anti-social, more like a nervous animal, avoiding by instinct those who would hurt his mind, wound his body, and deprive him of his small cache of treasures. His home becomes a blot on the landscape, noisome, shunned.

In such insanitary conditions lived Old Mick in the bounds of Huntlygate Farm, on the outskirts of Lanark, in 1952. Michael Connelly, aged 79, was thought to have come over from Ireland at the turn of the century. Ugliness crouched in a corner of a mead. His tumbledown shack, six feet by four, propped up by branches, was open-sided and little more than a field-shelter for beasts. Corrugated iron, now thought somewhat chic, was a part of the construction, and dangling sacking, when not thrown up, provided a curtaining when needed over the yawning open wall.

There was nothing cosy about this primitive private place, but Old Mick felt safe inside and had been living in this manner for at least 15 years. However, he was not such a hermit that he could not stir forth every Friday to collect his pension in Lanark, where he was well-known by sight. Nor did he eschew the public houses, but no one said that he was an alcoholic – which could, otherwise, have been at the root of his problems. His past had been as if carved away. His recent, known, history had begun that 15 years previously, in 1932, when Tom Alexander had taken over the farm together with Old Mick, who had done labouring work for the previous owner, with the shack thrown in.

The Alexanders liked the old man well enough and were quite happy to let him stay on their land, although he was by now too old to work. They did find him cantankerous. Tom Alexander only spoke to him once a week when he came to the farmhouse door, begging for scraps of food. Mrs Alexander had never had occasion to exchange words with him, and it was a mystery to her how he existed at all. In fact, he was a mystery to everyone as he trundled around the lanes, wrapped in his solitariness.

We might well wonder, with our enlightened views about care in the community if Old Mick's case was a triumph of that system, since he was certainly happier in his destitution than he would ever have been in a residential home. In those backward, old-fashioned days, the local authority social work department was well aware of his plight and repeatedly offered to place him in sheltered accommodation. His behaviour did not merit compulsory removal and he was still active and pursuing his own routine. It was, no doubt, a borderline case. As time passed and he became more helpless, the social workers would have had to step in. Probably they were his only visitors, met with abuse.

On Sunday, August 24th, 1952, a sizzling hot day, at noon, two boys walking in the lea came across the shack, and there, crumpled over a box of fruit, was the body of Old Mick, his head horrifically battered. He was facing inwards and had been hit from behind. For one whole week he had been dead and not missed, last seen alive on Friday, August 15th, presumably when he drew his pension. The police found sad relics of his life – a torn Catholic bible, one old pipe, two shabby spectacle cases, and an ancient candlestick.

The murder weapon was a lemonade bottle: the broken bottle neck, speckled with blood, lay beside the corpse and a rusty chisel could also have been used. There was a bloodstained towel. One set, and one set only of footprints going into and out of the shack, was discovered. No cash was hidden away and theft of the pension money was the obvious motive. Hermits attract thieves, like flies to rotten fruit.

The following morning, the murder was the talk of Lanark, and a certain young woman felt compelled to go to the police to tell them about George Francis Shaw, a 25-year-old Irish labourer with flashy good looks, the father of her three children. She could not understand how he could have been in a position to give her £2 on Sunday, August 17th, since he had been out of work for a fortnight after losing his job at a farm in the district, and the regular maintenance which he paid her was never that much. She had felt quite touched, at the time, but now she had a terrible suspicion.

That evening, Superintendent Hendry tracked Shaw down in a bar and took him in for questioning. He admitted that on Friday, August 15th, he and his friend, George Dunn, a farm worker, aged 22, also from Ireland , had met an old man on the bridge on the Lanark-Carstairs road. Dunn, not he, had hung back and spoken to him briefly before running on to catch up Shaw. No, definitely not, never, said Shaw, he did not know Old Mick, even though he himself had lived in Lanark for two years. He had never been to the shack. Hotly he denied that he had been anywhere near Huntlygate Farm on the weekend of 16th-17th August. Brightly there burned in Hendry's mind the knowledge that two young men had been seen on Friday, the 15th, boarding the Carstairs bus at the Huntlygate Farm stop.

Leaving it there for the moment, the superintendent had George Dunn brought in. He immediately owned to knowing Old Mick, and kept asking if Shaw had been arrested. A difficulty was beginning to show up in the investigation. The superintendent realized that Dunn was 'simple' and questioned him with caution, accordingly. Further enquiries were made, and it turned out that Shaw had been spotted with Dunn in a hotel in Lanark on August 17th. Shaw was flush with cash and bought a round of drinks. Later, at the cinema, he and Dunn talked to a 17-year-old girl, offering her cigarettes from a silver case.

Now to a detail which is ludicrous and inexplicable, yet profoundly incriminatory. During interviews, the police discovered that both young men were wearing Old Mick's socks. Somehow, by some unguessable means, the officers had found out that the old man had owned two pairs of socks – one on, one for washing in the ditch, presumably – and his corpse was *sans* socks.

Shaw and Dunn were charged with the murder, and Shaw, the 'normal' man, was interrogated continuously for a week, but would not confess. Superintendent Hendry put the comprehensive question, 'You struck him on the face and hands with a brick, iron bar and bottle, robbed him of two pairs of socks and a sum of money, didn't you?' 'No, that is not true,' Shaw insisted. All that Dunn would say was 'Ask Francis' (i.e. Shaw). Even when told that, as had been established, the single pair of footprints to and from the shack matched the hobnails on his boots, he looked blank and said again, 'Ask Francis.'

George Shaw and George Dunn were brought up for trial at the High Court in Glasgow in December. Counsel for the Crown stated that he did not intend to show which of the defendants actually killed the old man. In law, if each knew that the other intended at least serious violence to the victim, or one incited the other, then both were equally guilty of murder. In 1849, it was laid down that 'If they joined in reckless assault upon the party – reckless whether he live or die – and the party be killed, all joining are guilty, though it is proved that one particular blow caused the death, and though it cannot be proved by whom the particular blow was struck. If united in a murderous and brutal assault, all are responsible.'

Shaw's counsel stated at the outset that since he understood that it would be argued for Dunn that he was mentally abnormal, and therefore not fit to stand trial, his client, Shaw, should be tried separately, later on. This was disallowed, and the joint trial proceeded. The medical evidence was that Dunn had a mental age of eight and would be easily led by a stronger personality. Dr Thomas Curran stated that he was 'feeble-minded'. Dr Angus McNiven, who had assessed him in prison, was of the same opinion, further defining the case by saying that the diagnosis was not of insanity, but that the degree of mental impairment meant that Dunn could not understand the difference between right and wrong *as a normal person would*. This seems very fair, since Dunn would certainly have known that battering an old man to death would not be approved of, but the mind assessing what was going on was not a mature one. Dr David Anderson, medical officer at Barlinnie Prison, stated unequivocally that Dunn had no sense of moral responsibility, was illiterate, and did not appear to understand the gravity of the charge.

A bread salesman was brought by the Crown to testify that, in the June, Old Mick had told him that he had enough money for his own funeral without being a burden to anyone. George Shaw was put in the witness box. He said that he had been *near* Huntlygate Farm on the day *before* the murder, but that he and Dunn had spent the day in Carstairs on the Saturday. This seems like routine wiliness, but which *was* the actual day of the killing? Old Mick was last seen on the Friday, and two young men had been seen boarding the bus at the farm on the

Friday. Shaw and Dunn were flashing money around on the Sunday. On the face of it, the murder could have been committed at any time from Friday to Sunday between the markers. So why was Shaw so sure that the Saturday was the time to place himself elsewhere? Anyway, he was unable to provide an actual alibi, which might not have mattered too much, except that the police had been to Carstairs to enquire and no-one had even seen two young men in the village.

Both defendants were found Guilty of murder, by a majority of 11-3. The jury foreman stated that they considered that Dunn was indeed 'feeble-minded', and the judge ordered that he was to be detained in the asylum at Carstairs. This left George Shaw alone and exposed, and he was sentenced to be hanged. He appealed. The Lord Justice-Clerk presided at the six-day hearing and many and learned were the arguments. George Dunn had declined his right to appeal. There was a lack of direct evidence. Their lordships felt that whoever had robbed the old man must have killed. The socks were important. The appeal failed. Shaw joked like a jackass as he was led away with his boot-black hair gleaming. 'Right, boys, make it a good one!' he told the press photographers.

He did not meet the hangman, Albert Pierrepoint, with the same joke at Barlinnie Prison on January 26th, 1953. His last words were said to be, 'I am as innocent as anyone,' which could, in the case of a better brain, have been some deep, philosophical insight along the lines of guilt, but was, no doubt, an idiomatic means of emphasis. Some tender hearts felt uneasy. There were notional variations of the series of events at the shack. Anyway, a psychopath and a simpleton had hit a defenceless old hermit on the head, himself eccentric if not mad, and approaching senility. He had not put his trust in mankind, and he was proved right.

CHAPTER 8
THE LIGHT-HEADED CUTTY

In terms of caricature, which express a loathing of her unnatural act, Mrs Mary Smith's own counsel described her as a beaky character, 'like a vindictive masculine witch'. Sir Walter Scott stood further back and saw 'a face to do or die, or perhaps to do to die. Thin features, which had been handsome, a flashing eye, an acute and aquiline nose, lips much marked, as arguing decision, and, I think, bad temper – they were thin and habitually compressed, rather turned down at the corners, as one of a rather melancholy disposition.'

Mrs Smith was indeed much studied, an unsympathetic figure in the dock, as she conjured up a smokescreen of doubt to veil her deeds, and all in court searched for the truth hidden behind that strong, hawkish face. I have not yet said that the Wife o' Denside, as she was hymned in broadsheets, was actually to walk free, the verdict Not Proven, but there was, as we shall see, explanation enough for the jury's quaint variance from the general reception of the evidence.

The case was a wonder at the time, and widely argued. They spoke of little else in Dundee. The charge was that during one autumnal week in 1826, with full murderous intent, Mrs Smith had administered arsenic to her servant-girl, Margaret Warden, under the guise of attempting to procure an abortion. The girl died, and the foetus perished within her.

The cruelty took place in a fine rural setting, a working

farm wherein thoughts of the beauties of nature had no relevance, only profit, stark gain from grain and roots and the suffering of beasts. By extension of the 'pathetic fallacy' of literature, the environment of a murder can, traditionally, reflect and intensify its horror. If there were no evocation of the environment, a true crime writer's account would be considered 'bare' and at a disadvantage in a comparison with the embroidery of untrue crime writers.

Where the murder is exceptionally horrible to contemplate, there is an element of softening the reality by merging it into the greater scene. Older writers tended to expatiate too far on the grace and grandeur of certain settings, until relevance was lost. Enough to say that the farm at West Denside, in the county of Forfar, stood on an eminence in a field facing south to the Firth of Tay, with panoramic views of Dundee, estuary, sea, and the Bell Rock Lighthouse. The house, a low, crouching building of one storey under a grey slate roof, was fronted by a terrace from which a flight of steps led down to fields, later to a garden girdled by a high boxwood hedge.

Farmer David Smith, a remote figure, older than his wife and quite possibly feared by her, unless that were one of her pretences, held a string of three farms: Dodd, East Denside, and West Denside, where he had chosen to reside. There was a goodly measure of prosperity, and driving ambition and greed for more. There were two sons, Alexander, the elder, and George, who were both employed on the farm. One daughter was married to the foreman, James Miller. Farm workers were of both sexes. Women were not exempt from toiling in the fields: the 20th century landgirls were not a new phenomenon. It was better than working in the mines. Tess of the d'Urbervilles hacked swedes, drew reeds, and fed the threshing machine.

Margaret Warden, a lassie of a 'passionate and impulsive temper', was employed indoors and outdoors, and she was allowed to sleep in the kitchen. She was never Mrs Smith's favourite, but there under sufferance, and, lately, under punishment. Her father had died when she was 15 years old, and the widow had been left in some destitution with one son and two daughters. Mrs Machan, a sister of Mrs Smith, had taken pity on the family, and used her influence to place young Margaret at Denside. Mrs Warden was eternally grateful to the Smiths. It was a matter of receiving charity gratefully. The social difference was very marked and Mrs Smith was known to be stuck-up at the best of times.

Greater, then, was the shame when, at the age of 21, Margaret gave birth to an illegitimate baby whose father was never revealed, which was born and reared at her mother's home at Baldovie. After a period of rehabilitation, the outcast was allowed back at Denside, again through the good offices of propitiatory Mrs Machan. With her sin ne'er forgotten, she laboured to restore her reputation.

Even greater, then, was the disgrace when, at the end of July, 1826, Mary Smith discovered that her treasured younger son, George, groomed for advancement, was receiving Margaret Warden's favours. Plans for wedlock seem to have hung in the air. Such was the baffled and bitter wrath of the Wife o'Denside that we may wonder – only guessing – if another member of her precious family had been the first to press or practise the arts of love upon the girl who was there and helpless. Later attempts were made to portray the situation as an 'Upstairs-Downstairs' seduction and aftermath, but these were much humbler circumstances. An old print of a swooning servant-girl in a decent, if plain, wooden bed with ample bed-linen is way off the mark. Margaret slept in the box bed in the alcove in the kitchen, and her fellow-servant, Jean Norrie, shared that primitive couch. There was little comfort and less privacy.

Love might find a way, but Mother soon found out. Someone told Mrs Smith. The story was that she discovered the couple *in flagrante delicto*, or some approximation thereto, in the shadow of the barn beside the house. Abuse, vituperation, poured from the widow's thin, acid mouth, and twice betrayed, doubly defenceless, Margaret fled to her mother's cottage. There she was ill-received and again reviled, and returned to Denside. After a bare fortnight, she was back with her mother. Within a week, Mrs Smith drove over in the trap which she used to take her dairy produce for sale in Dundee and tried to persuade Margaret to go with her to that town to see a doctor. Margaret refused.

It was high summer and typhus and cholera were rife in the district and Mrs Warden somehow thought that avoiding disease was Mrs Smith's design. She assured her that her daughter had been bled quite recently and was no risk to herself or anyone else. Mrs Smith had other preoccupations, suspicious as she was that Margaret was with child, and hot for certainty.

'What do you think is wrong with Margaret?' she asked now cautiously as Mrs Warden walked her politely to her trap, but the widow 'didna ken'.

'I wish she binna wi' bairn,' Mrs Smith said threateningly.

'That is best known to herself' – the mother was discreet.

Mrs Smith was annoyed: 'If Margaret is in that condition, it will bring disgrace both upon you and me.'

And so she departed with her cheeses, saying that she was going to see the doctor in Dundee, to get something for herself, and something for Margaret, too. She must have put on a kind and helpful face, because, that night, Margaret returned to Denside and never set foot outside its boundaries again. She was under strict orders to keep her now finished relationship with George a secret from Mr Smith, whose wrath would have been terrible. By this time, the suspected pregnancy must have become a reality, because the girl allowed her mistress to dose her with potions which she believed were abortifacient. She was a passive, fatalistic victim, entirely dominated by an older woman who was fierce, and wheedling. Unwanted at her mother's home, she clung to the commanding presence of her employer, seeing no alternative. She 'often' confided in Jean Norrie that she was getting 'things' from Mrs Smith.

Certain timings do indicate that murder, not abortion, was the plan, *ab initio*. As we have said, Mrs Smith first discovered the liaison at the end of July. Margaret was permanently back at the farm some three weeks later. And on Monday, August 21st, Mrs Smith first took measures to obtain poison for rats. Dr William Dick, surgeon of Dundee, had been on friendly terms with the Smith family for many years. He had known Mrs Smith for 40 years (she was now 42) and considered her to be of 'humane character', liberal to her poor neighbours. (Another Mary McKinnon!) In the past, not recently, he had observed that she was prone to 'hysteria'.

On the 21st, two of his daughters visited Mrs Smith at Denside, and she told one of them to ask her father to make up some rat poison for her, saying that she would call for it herself the following Friday. Miss Dick forgot to deliver the message, and for some rather intriguing reason, Mrs Smith waited until September 1st before calling on Dr Dick. The interview, well remembered by the doctor, took place in his kitchen at noon. Quite openly, she accosted him: 'You have forgotten my poison for rats – the poison I sent the message about – I was so annoyed with rats.' Did she not have any cats? Yes, but she was no better for them. If it would oblige her, he would get the poison from an apothecary's shop, since he had nothing suitable to hand, and he also needed some articles for his own use.

Out at David Russell's shop, he asked the shopman, Andrew Russell, to put up some arsenic for a friend. One ounce of oxide of arsenic (i.e. the white powder, 'white arsenic') was packaged and tied in double wrapping, both papers marked *arsenic* on one side and *poison* on the other. Back at his house, Dr Dick made it very clear to Mrs Smith that the powder was arsenic and instructed her how to mix it up with a little oatmeal with her own hands, or see it done, in case of accident. He bestowed on her, at her additional request, a 'small dose' of a laxative medicine, made up of 20 grains jalap and five grains calomel. Jalap, obtained from the dried tubercles of the climbing plant, *ipomoea purga*, was a favourite, if drastic purgative. Side effects were violent griping, nausea and vomiting. The dose varied from 10 to 60 grains. Calomel, a dull, white powder, was to offset the discomforts.

Mrs Smith drove back to her farmstead with her spoil. She was now fully equipped for murder, although there is always a bridge to cross between the means, and the using of it. The purgative may be a red herring. She had not obtained a sufficient quantity for an heroic attempt at inducing abortion by that agent. Her personal need for the stuff could have been genuine. Poisoners have, of course, been known to mask their acquisition with an innocent purchase, and some time later Mrs Smith did go to Mrs Jolly, druggist of Dundee, for one ounce of castor-oil, which might have had some white mustard with it. One ounce of castor-oil might constitute two doses, so that it is not a massive prescription. It was to be suggested that purgatives were employed as the vehicle for the arsenic. The victim would recognise the familiar, reassuring taste of jalap or castor-oil.

If, theoretically, Mrs Smith, at least at the beginning, intended only to induce abortion, brewing up remedies like a witch and drawing upon her countrywoman's lore, it is only fair to state that arsenic has been used as an abortifacient. Taylor's *Medical Jurisprudence* has, for example, a fatal case of a 22-year-old girl, over five months' pregnant, who had been advised by someone to take a large dose of arsenic, which did not even have the desired effect.

The harvest of 1826 had been early, and much of the corn had already been cut, but there was one field of oats, immediately in front of the farmhouse on its sheltering eminence, which had been slower than the rest to ripen. This was the arena chosen by Mrs Smith as a physical ordeal for Margaret Warden, which certainly made the girl think that Mistress was helping her to get rid of the baby. Together with Ann and Agnes Gruar, she was set to shearing the field, and she was seen forking the corn with a will, like Ruth, gleaning in the fields of barley. Mrs Smith had told her that a régime of fasting and hard work, in conjunction with what she would be giving her, would do the trick. Nothing is heard of the young swain, George, who must have witnessed the activities, unless his mother had found an excuse to banish him.

On Monday, September 4th, however, her strength failed and she sat down by the ungathered sheaves and confided her miseries to her two companions. She said that 'She was not able for her work, must leave Denside, and did not know where to go because she would rather take her own life than endure the cruelty of her relatives.' She threatened to 'put an ill end to herself'. 'God keep me!' said Ann Gruar, and went away in fear. There is a legend, apparently a mere tale, although it would have been in character, that at this moment, the Wife o' Denside glided over from the house and offered the wilting girl a flagon of tea, which revived her.

On the Tuesday, she toiled all day without complaint, and, in the evening, fell asleep in a chair by the fire while Jean Norrie was working around the kitchen. When it was the girls' usual bedtime, at 10 o'clock, and they were sitting by the ingle, Mrs Smith came in from the parlour with a glass of liquid, which she kept stirring with a spoon. It was a pretty large dram-glass, about full. Saying that she had already taken her share, she administered one spoonful to Jean – straight into her mouth – and gave the rest, in the glass, to Margaret and the girl drank it in one go. Then she presented Margaret with a lump of sugar.

Jean said that the liquid was 'white-like'. It did not taste of castor-oil, which her mistress had given her once before. She had seen cream of tartar in the past, and that was what it really looked like. The girls clambered into their bed in the cupboard and slept. The next morning, when Jean woke up, she found Margaret, nauseous, weakly trying to light the fire. She was cold and shivering. Jean helped her back to bed and then had to leave her, to work outside. At dinner-time, she was still in bed and sorry for herself. In the evening, she was prostrate, with a 'sore side' and internal pains.

'Oh!' she said, taking hold of her friend's hands. 'What I ha'e bidden [suffered] this day!'

'Have the Smiths been owning [looking after] you?'

'Rather too weel.'

Jean mentioned the Grim Reaper, and Margaret said, 'Some fowk wad be glad o' that.'

That night, the two girls shared the bed again, uncomfortably, and Jean found Margaret wide-awake in the early morning. All day long she vomited and purged and begged for water, which she could not retain. All day long she cried for her mother, but Mrs Smith told her, 'Wheesht and haud your tongue till your physic operate,' and brought her yet more 'castor-oil'. Would whisky help poor Margaret? (she asked Jean Norrie.)

'She has got enough of that, or something else,' the servant replied, 'for such purging and vomiting I never saw.'

Mrs Smith went away, vexed. 'Say nothing to her about it,' Margaret begged. She whispered to Jean that Mistress had burned her inside with whisky. Jean urged her to take no more of the drinks. 'Mistress says they're good for the "wheezle" in my breath.' 'Dinna tell me it's your breath. I ken better!' said Jean, and Margaret murmured then, 'I ken ither things, too.'

On Friday, Margaret was drowsy and 'queer-like'. Jean Norrie, in close proximity, was only too well-placed to witness her inexorable decline. Faintly, the dying girl said, 'You ken, Jean, wha has been the occasion o' me lyin' here?'

'No,' said Jean.

'Dinna say naething.'

'Dinna *you* say naething,' said Jean, 'for I dinna ken.'

'They'll get their rewards.'

'If it's onybody you're blamin', you'll surely forgi'e them,' and Margaret agreed that she would.

'I've told you before no to tak ony mair o'thae drinks the mistress gi'ed you.'

At last, Margaret's mother was at her bedside. When Jean was out of the room, she asked her daughter, 'Has onybody given you onything, or has onybody hurt you?' This seems a plain enough suspicion, and one would not put it past Mrs Smith to attempt abortion with an instrument.

'My mistress ga'e me it,' was Margaret's reply. Her mother felt 'so sorry' and 'there was naething more said on the subject.' The girl was crying out in great pain and 'burning'. Her mother felt her hands. They were cold as the coffin and Margaret said pitifully that they 'wad be caulder yet.'

At last, a doctor was called. It was the mother, not Mrs Smith, who summoned Dr Taylor, of Broughty Ferry. He arrived at noon on that Friday. Mrs Smith was at the door, 'knitting her stocking', a picture of nonchalance. She took him into her parlour and told him that her servant had been ill with vomiting and pain in her bowels, ever since Tuesday. Why had he not been sent for sooner? Because, said the spidery one, 'She was not aware that her complaint was so serious, and she was a light-headed cutty[1] and they had not paid that attention to her that they might have done.' She had given her nothing but castor-oil during the course of the illness. Then Mrs Smith asked a curious question. It was reported that the girl was with child: would the doctor know so if he saw her? Very likely, he told her, with some irony. Was

1 'Flighty little trollop' would seem to convey the spirit of the description.
'Cutty' is usually given as 'a short stump of a girl', sometimes used playfully.

it not likely, she persisted, that the vomiting and purging would carry off the child, if there were one? She confided in him that a baby 'would be a stain on the family'.

Why was she saying all this to the doctor? Was she still not sure that there *was* a pregnancy? Was she trying to guide his thoughts along the lines of an attempted abortion, howsoever effected, or by whom, in order to distract him from graver suspicions? Dr Taylor was beginning to dislike the direction of the discussion, anyway, and said shortly that he had come for the purpose of seeing the patient, and did not choose to indulge in such conversation.

He was taken to the kitchen, where he found Margaret Warden just coming out of a fit of vomiting. She looked very ghastly and fell over, almost insensible. The heartbeat was indistinct and rapid – 150 to 160 a minute. He could detect no pulse at the wrist or temples. The extremities were perfectly cold, and there was a cold perspiration all over the body. The arms had a dark appearance. He tried to rouse the girl, but the simplest question exhausted her, and he did not feel justified in continuing. He said later that, 'I understood her to be with child for about three months. She said nothing from which I could infer that she had done herself ill.'

The doctor finished his examination, and Mrs Smith drew him back into her parlour. What did he think of Warden? The straight answer was that she would be dead in a few hours' time. He did not prescribe any medicine, because he made it a rule not to prescribe for a dying patient. Mrs Smith merely remarked that she had sent for a medical man to take the responsibility off her own shoulders. Was there a pregnancy, then? The doctor said that he had every reason to believe so. The vomiting and purging might displace it, or, on the other hand, might not. Mrs Smith commented that 'she would take care, though, that it did, as the gudeman [her husband] would tear down the house about her'. I think that this should have been reported as 'she would *not* care'. She would hardly have told the doctor that she was contemplating some positive action to encourage miscarriage. The doctor departed. Mrs Smith need not have worried, because he was under the impression that it was a fatal case of cholera.

After three days of unalleviated suffering, at 9 o'clock on the evening of Friday, September 8th, 1826, Margaret Warden expired. As the grieving mother and friends saw to her body, they marvelled at its dark colouration. Next day, Mrs Margaret Smith, the farmer's sister-in-law, called to enquire. She asked if it was the fever that Warden had died of, and Mrs Smith said that was right. The girl had been in the family way, she (our Mrs Mary Smith) had heard, but personally, she did not believe it. Why was the body blue? Oh! The doctor had advised her that all who died of the fever were blue. (Dr Taylor did not corroborate that exchange, and he was to repudiate a later assertion by Mrs Smith that he had intimated that the illness was 'water in the chest' – i.e. probably left ventricular failure.)

Although the down-trodden, eleemosynary mother was too intimidated by Mrs Smith to make any noises of discontent, she did tell her other daughter, in confidence, when they were 'coming to the coffining', what Margaret had said to her about her mistress. She did not tell her son, 'because it could not bring her back, and would fetch disgrace upon the Denside family'. Afterwards, she attributed her silence to gratitude to Mrs Machan, who had taken pity on her widowed state.

In haste, on the Sunday, two days after her death, Margaret Warden was buried in an aura of shame, not suspicion, in the kirkyard of Murroes. The coffin bore the brief inscription, *M.W., aged 25*. The rumours began within a week. Information was lodged with the Sheriff of Forfarshire, and the body was exhumed by his order on September 30th. They laid the mortal remains of the light-headed cutty' on a convenient, flat tombstone and carried out the post-mortem there and then. Carved on the stone underneath, an angel blew his last trump and the four deep occupants arose from their grave.

Dr Taylor was there as signs of a three to four month pregnancy were found. Portions of internal organs, which were well preserved, were removed and sent to the Crown Agent at Edinburgh for analysis to be arranged. Arsenic was present *passim*. Mrs Smith was summoned for judicial examination before Christopher Kerr, Sheriff-Substitute at Dundee, but, no longer capable of knitting her stocking, she announced herself prevented from the stress of travelling, by reason of sudden indisposition. The Procurator Fiscal, Dr John Boyd Baxter, appointed Dr Johnston of Dundee, one of the post-mortem physicians, to test her. If he considered that she was well enough to go with him, it was proposed that her precognition should be taken at an inn known as the Four Mile House, situated midway between Denside and Dundee.

On October 2nd, Dr Johnston examined Mrs Smith at her home and proclaimed her 'not in excellent health' but fit to meet the requirement. She was unwilling, but induced to travel in the chaise with him, supported by her husband and one of her sons. Not George, presumably. On the way, Mr Smith remarked bitterly that none of his friends could believe the rumours that had been spread abroad about his wife, and there must have been something more in the matter than he knew of, otherwise gentlemen would not be travelling about the country in carriages. He had heard that poison had been found in the stomach of the dead girl? That was the truth, the doctor assured him, and he trusted that none of his family had given it to her.

Unwisely, Mrs Smith piped up, 'Warden vomited so much before her death that I wouldn't have thought anything could have remained on her stomach.' Her husband hastily offered the suggestion that more than one of his servants had heard the girl say that she would put away with herself. In the lobby of the inn, when Dr Johnston was satisfied that Mrs Smith felt no worse, the judicial examination proceeded in due form. The husband was allowed to stay, and he made no objections. Mrs Smith was observed to be in her sound senses, quite calm and collected, until the last question was put to her, when she became agitated, gasped, and fell back on her chair, but as swiftly recovered.

This was the first of two statements, and it did not match Dr Taylor's recollections. She denied any knowledge of the girl's pregnancy before she died. Margaret was sometimes not well enough to work, and her difficulty in breathing had been worse in the week before her illness. She herself had asked the doctor if the girl was with child because she was of rather loose character. She had given her a dose of castor-oil at bedtime about a fortnight before she became ill, and just one more on the 4th or 5th of September. It was mixed with some lozenger wine[2] in a dram glass or tumbler. She had bought the castor-oil from Mrs Jolly on the previous Friday, together with some mustard and some 'Arnetta' for dyeing.

To her knowledge, she had never had any poisonous substances about the house except that two years ago a rat-catcher had been brought in and he might have used poison for all she knew. The only drug that she had bought at the relevant time came from Mrs Jolly of Dundee. As she answered the questions about drugs, this was the occasion when Mrs Smith dramatically lost her composure. Since both a medical practitioner and an apothecary were waiting in the wings to attest to her purchase of arsenic for rats, she had clearly blundered, but knew not how to escape other than by plain denial. They committed her that night to the Tolbooth in Dundee for further examination.

The following morning, Mrs Smith's pack of connections prevailed upon the Sheriff Substitute to meet the Fiscal in the

2 Not traced. I suppose you *could* steep lozenge sweets in water, or wine, and make a kind of sweet cordial. Or, as a long-shot: fake, i.e. non-alcoholic wine, from losenger (obs.) – a deceiver.

place of her confinement to take a second, voluntary statement from her. She wished to tell the truth and to make some corrections. She now recollected that on that crucial Friday she had acquired 'something to put away rats' from Dr Dick. She was not told that it was poison: there was some writing on it but she did not know what it said. She did not ask for arsenic. Mrs Dick advised her to put the stuff into the holes and craps of the walls, and she did that on the following Monday, inserting it into the crevices in the loft above the bothie. (Servants slept in the bothie, and a hen and chicks were kept in the loft.) Margaret Warden had been with her in the kitchen when she got a plate to mix it with meal. No other servant knew about it. Denside was infested with rats. If you went into the byre, they moved away in front of you like a drove of cattle. The servants complained that they disturbed their sleep.

Mrs Mary Elder or Smith was committed for trial on December 28th, 1826, before the High Court of Justiciary at Edinburgh. Those two leading lights of the Scottish bar, Francis Jeffrey and Henry Cockburn, were retained for the defence by the munificence of the stunned and outraged husband. On the day, however, the Lord Advocate moved for a postponement. He had learnt only the day before that the defence was that Margaret Warden had committed suicide and he understood that 48 witnesses were to be adduced in support of that contention. He needed time to examine those persons, by Scottish procedure.

The trial finally got off the ground on February 5th, 1827, but there was a jinx on it, because at 5.30pm, during the Crown evidence, one of the jurymen, Mr Thomas, blockmaker of Leith, fell into a fearsome epileptic fit, following the unearthly cry which sometimes presages a convulsion. It so happened that the expert witness thus interrupted in full flow was the famous Professor Christison, and he leapt like a mountain goat from the witness box to help the stricken, threshing man – all movement and disorder where formality and restraint should have prevailed. It was a most unusual scene. Other medical men present in court came forward to help, and Thomas was carried insensible into an adjoining room.

After an hour, he was still not fit to return, and Professor Christison gave formal evidence that although he was considerably recovered, a relapse might be expected and his memory was affected. The Lord Advocate was fast on his feet to submit that the jury should be discharged and a date set for a new trial. The hidden agenda was that the Crown was grasping at the chance of more time for preparation, having been put under pressure by the process called 'running criminal letters' which forced the prosecution to proceed within a limited period. Counsel for Mrs Smith would have none of it, and the Court met on February 12th for seven hours of argument, all the Lords of Justiciary attending. It was an important debate, the first occasion on which the legality of resuming a trial interrupted by the illness of a member of the jury had been determined. Mrs Smith was, as it were, half tried.

Eventually, on February 19th, a full new jury of 15 was empanelled and the case proceeded. When the Crown proposed that Mrs Smith's two damaging statements should be read out, her counsel objected to them, on the ground that she was subject to an 'hysterical affection' – a wandering and weakness of the mind – and that she was especially afflicted in that way before her first precognition. (This does not mean that her sanity was at issue.) The reading was deferred, and Jean Norrie was called. She 'remembered of Warden saying in the field one day when she was holing a pickle potatoes that she didna ken what to do and she wad surely do some ill to hersel' '. Jean did not believe that Margaret would do it, because she was 'a rash creature of her words'. She herself had been at Denside since Martinmas, 1825, and milked the cows in the byre, but had never seen a rat there. Her mistress did once tell her that she kept some King's yellow (orpiment i.e. sulphuret of arsenic) to poison the flies.

Mr Smith's sister-in-law described Mrs Smith's 'hysterics'. Once she had taken her out of church in that state, and the fit had made her insensible so that she forgot she had been in church and could not speak correctly, even the second day. (There is an organic tinge to these symptoms: surely there was not one epileptic in the jury box and another in the dock!)

The presence of droves of rats at the farm was a vital issue for the defence, in order to justify Mrs Smith's acquisition of arsenic and also to suggest an available means for Margaret Warden to kill herself, but the Crown brought a number of witnesses to deny sight of even a whisker at the relevant time. Rats had, probably, damaged the horse-harness, but that was 'last Whitsunday'.

Mr Lyon Alexander, surgeon of Dundee, was brought to show that Mrs Smith had been incompetent to make a true declaration. Called out in a great hurry to Denside on October 2nd, he had found her in a state of 'stupor and insensibility' and 'talking of persons as present who were not'. It appeared to be a 'violent nervous attack' and he did not consider that she was in a fit state to be examined on suspicion of having committed a crime. Temporary loss of memory would have been a feature. He had administered antispasmodics, and left. When he saw her the next evening, in prison, she was vague about what had passed the night before. Her friends told him that she had received a severe nervous shock during the day on hearing that a grandchild had nearly drowned. Another medical man, John Crichton, surgeon of Dundee, examined Mrs Smith in gaol, two months later, and found her in convulsions, foaming at the mouth with attendants applying hot flannels. If he could give the complaint a name, he would call it violent hysteria, approaching to epilepsy. She could not speak coherently, and in his considered opinion, she was not feigning the symptoms.

Unimpressed, the Court let in the two declarations, against which her counsel had fought a strong yet losing battle. In the end, though, they proved to have done her little harm. The case for the Crown was closed and the Defence began to call witnesses about rats. There was *no* parade of 48 witnesses to show Margaret Warden as a suicide. Andrew Murray, the rat-catcher referred to in Mrs Smith's second statement had been drawn to court by the inducement of a curious advertisement inserted in the *Dundee Advertiser* of January 25th: 'To the benevolent' it was headed, and it ran on: 'Andrew Murray, Rat-catcher is particularly requested to call at Mr Smith's, Farmer [etc.]. All his expenses will be paid.' Mr Smith, and his agents, MacEwan and Miller, writers in Dundee, also asked for information regarding a middle-aged woman, lately travelling in Fife, selling matches, accompanied by a ten-year-old boy carrying, like Marcel Proust seen entering a brothel, a white mouse in a box.

Murray testified that he had *left* some rat poison, consisting of arsenic, anise (aniseed), and oatmeal at Denside when he had been there 'in the way of business' some three and a half years previously. Two years later, he had been to the Mill of Affleck, then owned by Mr Smith, and had left some medicine with Mrs Smith at that time. Called in by the advertisement, he had recently found traces of vermin at Denside – 'the small Scots rat, and mice siclike' – but he had not actually seen any. It does seem that Murray was scarcely worth the advertisement, and damaging, to boot.

Mrs Hamilton, an itinerant pedlar of odds and ends, was the wanted woman, and she, too, had been persuaded to testify that she knew Margaret Warden well. She had been a frequent caller at Denside, where Mrs Smith had allowed her to sleep in the barn. Margaret had confided in her, weeping and imploring. What was she to do, being not able for her work, and she had got rough usage from her own mother and brother on a former occasion? Come, now, the pedlar had comforted her, a mother's heart was aye kindly, and she would be the first to pity her. No, no, the girl had said, she would be tossed and handled in the way she was before and she would put an end to herself.

The boy with the mouse in the cage was not produced, but Mrs Smith's agents had found Robert Easson, merchant of Broughty Ferry, who remembered that a boy had come to his shop on the Monday or Tuesday of the week in which Margaret died, and asked for twopence-worth of arsenic, which was refused. The implication was, of course, that the girl had sent him on that errand.

The tests as proving the presence of arsenic were attacked with great fire by the defence. It was a rehearsal for the later great arsenic trials such as Madeleine Smith. There was, too, the matter of yellow particles found in the deceased's stomach, where white arsenic might have been expected. Professor Christison considered that white arsenic might have been converted into the yellow, sulphuretted form by a chemical process after death. (The reader may recall that in my previous volume, *Scottish Murder Stories* p.54, I said that I had searched in vain for such a case, although I had learnt from *Taylor* that the change was known to occur.) The yellow specks did not benefit Mrs Smith, anyway, because she had admitted to Jean Norris that she had 'King's yellow' in her possession.

Calm and collected, showing no signs of hysteria or epilepsy, she sat like a thinking statue, listening to all the evidence. The Lord Advocate began his closing speech at 11 o'clock at night, and he spoke for two hours. As the day died and the lights were brought, one of the candles placed on the rim of the dock flickered in a cross-draught and ran down unevenly on one side, whereupon Mrs Smith coolly kept lifting the candle and turning it round.

Sir William Rae came to the matter of the rats, and mentioned that Murray's small, black Scots rat was, in fact, extremely rare in Scotland! If, he went on, it were argued that Mrs Smith was only guilty of an attempt to procure abortion, the word 'arsenic' alone was a sufficient answer: no one could use that without a deadly purpose. (That, however, as we have seen, was not always the case.) The dead girl's rank in life precluded the notion that she had felt her shame to be worse than life. (An interesting social comment, but the better view, if pushing for suicide, was surely that she despaired because she felt abandoned by all who should have cared for her.)

It was a weakness in the Crown case that there was a vagueness attached to the exact times of the administration of arsenic, not to mention the quantity, and Jeffrey, for Mrs Smith, vigorously milked this grey area. His speech lasted for another two and a half hours. He asked the jury to marvel at the calm and cheerful manner in which his client had ministered to the dying girl, day after day. (But that, of course is the art and conduct of the classic poisoner.) He referred to Mrs Smith's previous good character. He still clung to the original diagnosis of cholera and pooh-poohed the wonders of science – blunders, more likely. Six witnesses had spoken of suicide. Rats there *were* at Denside. Mystery befogged the case. Not Proven would be the just verdict.

By now, it was 3 o'clock in the morning. The jury had been listening for 18 hours. When the judge began his charge, they struggled to their feet, but, contrary to custom, they were not told to resume their seats and were forced to stand for two and a half hours. Such a feat of endurance was thought to have coloured their response to the judge's admonitions. The Lord Justice-Clerk summed up against Mrs Smith, and when their ordeal was over, the jury expressed a wish to retire. They returned the following afternoon with a unanimous verdict of Not Proven. It was an unpopular result, and feelings ran high.

Lord Cockburn in 1838, upon reading Lockhart's *Life of Scott*, recorded in his diary these words: 'Lockhart mentions Scott as having gone to see my old client, Mrs Smith, who was guilty, but acquitted, of murder by poison … Sir Walter's remark upon the acquittal was: "Well, sirs, all I can say is, that if that woman was my wife, I should take good care to be my own cook!" '

CHAPTER 9
THE POSTMAN ONLY KNOCKED ONCE

The watcher in the bracken had made himself a kind of deer's 'harbour' or bed, but it was the tactics of warfare, not stalking, that he was employing. Since the hours of darkness, possibly all night, he had been waiting patiently. He was armed with a sawn-off shotgun, and he was wearing overalls. His lair was close enough – a few hundred yards – to the house in the Highlands for him to be able to calculate exactly when all the members of the McIntyre family had gone out, except for Catherine, a housewife of 47, left all on her own and unprotected, expecting no sudden inrush of evil. Too close, and the Cairn terrier could have scented his adrenaline, and become suspicious. If only a more formidable dog had been around the place …

The husband, head shepherd on the Tombuie Estate, went off to work very early. The two daughters, Annie and Mary, were, in fact, on holiday in the Isle of Arran. Archie, the son, also a farm worker, said goodbye at about 8.00am, and as he walked along the road, he actually saw a movement in the four-foot-high bracken but thought that it was probably one of the deer. He walked on. The watcher had made a mistake, and, if challenged, he could well have used that gun.

An alien predator loose in the peaceful countryside, Stanislaw Myszka, aged 23, was a deserter from the Polish Army in Exile. For a time, he had been resident at Taymouth Castle, by the shores of Loch Tay, near Kenmore, in Perthshire, which was in use as a resettlement centre for some

800 Polish soldiers who elected to stay in Britain after the war and build up new lives. They were beginning to find Scottish wives.

Tower Cottage, the McIntyres' home, set high on the slopes of Bolfracks Hill above Loch Tay, could be seen from the castle. It was not an ordinary Highland cottage, being built in parts of differing design and materials around a stumpy, machiolated watchtower, once, by the look of it, a small fortress, but now far from impregnable. Myszka was undoubtedly familiar with the cottage and the nature of its occupants. Local knowledge must have drawn him there to its special feature – McIntyre was holding £90 in cash in readiness to pay it out in wages to the under-staff on the estate.

That Friday, 26th September, 1947, Catherine McIntyre did not stop to wash up the breakfast dishes when her husband and son had gone, because she wanted to write a letter to her daughters before the postman called at 10.00am. He would take the letter away with him, since the isolated house was nowhere near a postbox. In the afternoon, she was going out to have tea with her friend, Mrs McKerracher, whose husband had a neighbouring farm. Her day was mapped out pleasantly. She sat down at the table in the kitchen and began to write …

Outside, the Polish soldier began to run and duck down the hill. He got to the door and knocked. The terrier yapped. Or perhaps he just burst in. He flourished his shotgun. His primary intent might have been robbery with whatever violence proved necessary and his victim may have hoped to survive. When he had finished, he returned to his lair and cleaned himself up as well as he could. The bloodied overalls came off and his brand new suit went on. It was thought that it was at this stage, not earlier, that he gave himself a 'dry-shave' and threw the razor-blade into the bracken. He decamped, with his spoils.

At 10.00am, the postman called. There was no reply when

he knocked, so he left the McIntyres' two newspapers on the step and continued on his round. At 5.15pm, Archie came home for his tea. The doors were locked, the dog was barking furiously outside and the newspapers were still on the step. He remembered that his mother had been planning to go out visiting, and thought that she must have been delayed for some reason. He sat down on the doorstep and began to read one of the newspapers. At 5.30pm, McKerracher appeared, somewhat worried, saying that Mrs McIntyre had never turned up for tea. They wondered if she had had an accident in the house.

Archie fetched a ladder and climbed through the kitchen window. All was silent, and wrong. The breakfast dishes were still in the scullery sink, unwashed, and the letter to the girls lay, unfinished, on the table, stopped in mid-sentence. He searched the first floor, then the second, calling for his mother. The door to his own bedroom was locked, which did not make sense. He fetched an axe and broke the door down. Mother was lying dead on one of the beds in his room, with a mattress taken from another bed squashed on top of her body. Her hands and feet were tightly tied with black bootlaces, and she had been gagged with a scarf. Finally, her head had been severely battered in a murderous attack.

The police were called out. Blunt old black cars began to mass outside the towered cottage. One of Archie's suits had been stolen from his wardrobe and the shepherds' wages had gone, of course. Archie recalled the movement in the bracken, and the hideout, sown with its clues, was quickly discovered. The razor-blade was there, and part of a bloodstained handkerchief. Nearby, a local constable found the shotgun, in pieces, with the butt stained with blood; two cartridges; and a pair of overalls covered with blood. Also found, was a railway ticket stamped Perth to Aberfeldy, dated for the previous day, which was identified by railway officials as of the type issued only to soldiers in uniform. Taymouth Castle immediately sprang to mind, and, using a team of interpreters, the police began to question all the Polish soldiers who had been billeted at the centre.

There was no description of a suspect to go on, but details of the shotgun were broadcast, and a gardener who lived at Old Meldrum, in Aberdeenshire, thought that he recognized it. He had recently lent just such a gun to a farm grieve, who had found it missing when he wanted to use it. The police went to interview the gardener and the grieve, and learnt that a Pole named Stanislaw Myszka had been employed on the farm there, before moving south to Perth in search of a new job, during the week of the murder. After a few days, he had returned to Old Meldrum with a new suit, and he seemed to be in funds, although there was no sign of a job. The grieve and his wife identified the fragment of a bloodstained handkerchief as part of one which they had given to the Pole.

A taxi driver might have carried Myszka from Aberfeldy to Perth: he remembered a foreigner who looked as if he had been sleeping rough and paid his fare from a thick roll of banknotes. This could have been the same man who had been spotted coming out of a wood, before taking a bus to Aberfeldy. A girl from Ardallie, newly married to one of the Polish soldiers based at Taymouth Castle, reported that a friend of theirs, called Stanislaw Myszka, who had been chronically short of money, had suddenly taken them on a shopping spree.

The now named fugitive was caught by two constables after a chase through a disused RAF airfield at Longside, near Peterhead, where he had been sleeping in one of the disused huts. The photograph of Myszka under arrest, in handcuffs, shows a very young, small, pinched, ratty man, hunched and stumbling, wearing a large, pale cap and a strained, striped suit of 'demob' cut, obviously not his. At the police station, Catherine McIntyre's gold wedding ring was found hidden in his shoe.

Professor John Glaister conducted the post-mortem at Perth. His findings were that 'Death resulted from fracture of the base of the skull, with subdural haemorrhage, the result of very considerable violence, together with superimposed respiratory embarrassment.' There were four deep lacerated wounds on the head. Beard hairs were noticed on the razor-blade which Myszka had discarded in the bracken. Professor Glaister had a special interest in hair and had indeed published *A Study of Hairs*, in 1931. He asked for samples of Myszka's shaved hairs to be brought to him from Perth Prison and compared them, mounted on slides, with the original shaved hairs. All were fair to very light brown and 'their gross and detailed structural characteristics matched'. Before DNA, it was only possible to state that hairs were 'consistent with a common source'. Hair was not so accurate as fingerprints for purposes of identification. The perameters of its use were carefully defined at Myszka's trial at Perth.

The special defence of insanity had been lodged but it was an uphill struggle because this was a clear murder for gain. Possibly there was an element of mental disturbance in the man due to war trauma, loss and deprivation, and *anomie* in a foreign land, but of course his compatriots at the Castle had suffered similar misfortunes and they had not gone on the rampage. It was said that he had been made ill by worry after hearing that his children, who had been living in France, were to be repatriated to Poland. He was hanged at Perth on February 6th, 1948.

CHAPTER 10
BRUTALITY

'**T**arzan' was what they called James Keenan around the streets of Lanark in 1969. It must have been said ironically, because, although he went in for weight-lifting and was presumably strong and muscled, he was a small man, about five feet tall. One feels that his size was a formative element of his personality, as evidenced by his choice of a compensatory hobby. In his photograph, which is very striking, he does not look like a murderer, his face fine and thin, his eyes very dark, melancholy, a Chatterton one could have believed, without knowledge.

His relatives, as reported, all concurred on the harmony of his marriage. At the time of the tragedy, people who knew the couple seemed to be reluctant to speak out. Someone must have been aware that they were disagreeing over the upbringing of their child – if that, offered by Keenan, were the real source of trouble – and someone must have suspected that he had a short fuse. Not that anyone outside the vortex could have prevented the outcome. The crime was said to have been out of character but that is the nature of matrimonial murder! 'The privacy of marriage is a shocking thing. We try to present our own, particularly if we are women, in a good light, or, if men, in no light at all. We struggle not to listen to the secrets of other people's marriages. Thus marriages live in isolation, sometimes becoming, for want of compassion and criticism, more bizarre, more cruel, more wild or more eccentric, than any of us can possibly imagine.' (In Hilary Bailey's *Mrs*

Mulvaney.) There does seem to be a measurable period of premeditation in fetching an axe and killing your wife with it. An argument over the correct way to bath the baby scarcely seems provocation for such a brutal murder.

The small family lived in a council house at 40 Wellwood Avenue, Lanark. Keenan was 35 years old, and his wife, Elizabeth, was 29. They had been married for some 11 years. Elizabeth had had to endure an ovarian operation in order to conceive a child. Having such a procedure in the 1960s must be an indication of how much the wife, and perhaps the husband, wanted a baby. A 14-month-old girl had not brought the happiness that had been expected. Her name was published at the time, but it is kinder not to perpetuate the sadness. James Keenan had not, of late, been doing very well: he had been out of work for several months, and he had been losing money on the horses. Finance was, therefore, another source of stress at home. He liked a drink, but was not an alcoholic.

He attacked his wife on the night of Wednesday, March 19th, 1969. Elizabeth was last seen alive at home that evening, when her brother had called to ask if James would mind running his wife to hospital the next morning, to have a minor operation, since he was unemployed. Who knows if this rankled, but James agreed, and the brother-in-law left at about 7.30pm, when all seemed normal. The fatal matrimonial argument over bathing the baby flared up while Elizabeth was still dressed, and, by implication, at the baby's bath time. It could have happened very shortly after the relative had left and perhaps their supper had been put back, and they were hungry. If the row was actually in the bathroom, he must surely have gone out of the room to fetch the axe from kitchen, lobby, shed, yard... Even so, that was not time enough for cooling off to take place, apparently. Or had he been fantasizing about killing her?

Then Keenan drank a bottle of whisky and the next thing he remembered, he said, was seeing his wife in the bath, cut up into sections, and he with a hacksaw in his hand. He vomited. There were four parcels to pack: the legs, the torso with the arms intact, and the head. As his thoughts swung and gibbered in the jungle of his mind, he had no intention of giving himself up and concentrated on careful wrapping, in several layers. For this purpose he made the cardinal error of drawing upon materials occurring naturally in his own home environment: a cot blanket; unusually dark, heather-mixture blankets; a paper carrier bag; and so on.

He had the whole night in which to eliminate the signs of carnage, and he was just about as thorough as anyone could be in those circumstances, although it was probably not a good idea to leave the remains of a super-size container of scouring powder half-burnt in the ashes in the fireplace. It must have been smeared with blood. At some stage in the proceedings, he carried his heavy parcels outside and stowed them in the boot of his car. Formed and still forming in his brain were a series of subterfuges, errands and disposals. Everything depended on his manner, his ability to appear normal and act appropriately, in which he succeeded remarkably well – until he encountered Detective Chief Superintendent William Muncie, one week later.

The next morning, he took his now motherless child to his own mother's house, and presented himself at 10 o'clock as arranged at his sister-in-law's, appearing cool and detached, composed and caring, chatting with his mind on automatic pilot during the 14-mile journey to hospital, while behind him, the parcels were rolling around in the boot of his car. Straight on next to his mother-in-law's home to enact a prepared performance. 'Is she here?' he shouted, bounding up the stairs like a character in a farce.

The story which he had fabricated was that Elizabeth had walked out the night before after a quarrel when she had let the baby fall in the bath. No, she had not taken any clothes, but he had thrown some money at her as she left – about £50 or £60, which she had put in her purse. Mrs Elizabeth Roberts, her mother, was, naturally extremely worried about her daughter and at her request Keenan drove her to a relative's house to make, of course, fruitless enquiries. It was getting on for 5 o'clock in the afternoon, and he was anxious about the parcels. Politely declining to go on to another relative, he drove off on a circular or rather elliptical tour of disposal. He had too many obligations to range far and wide, but he did the best he could in the time available and was back, playing with his child later that evening.

The torso was dumped in a copse on Thankerton Moor, which had been the site of a prisoner of war camp. One leg was thrown from a bridge into the Water of Leith at Balerno and the other was dropped from a road bridge on to the Aberdeen to Edinburgh railway line, between the northbound tracks. The head was left in a large wood on the Lang Whang road, which runs from Lanark via Carnwath to Edinburgh.

Keenan did not report his wife as a mising person, adhering to his oft-told tale that he was the deserted party and that she had left of her own accord and would return when the money ran out. He moved into his mother-in-law's home as a lodger, saying that he could not bear to stay alone in his own house. His sister-in-law took in the child. He drank in his local public house and played dominoes, the very picture of a wronged man just waiting for everything to get back to normal again.

However, when the remains began to be found – and it did not take long – the situation changed. Until then, Elizabeth Keenan's family had been seething with anxiety, but not with suspicion. The legs came to light first, four miles apart, on March 24th, although, in fact, people had been wondering about the parcel wedged between stones in the middle of the river from the evening of the 21st onwards – so soon. The woman who finally reported it did so because she thought that it looked like a dead baby. The parcel on the railway tracks was, at first, taken to be a dead cat.

A murder squad was set up. Pathologists said that the woman had been well-nourished, a brunette, between 20 and 40 years old, and about five feet two inches in height. Bizarrely, the legs were still in nylon stockings – which showed that the attack had occurred before bedtime. James Keenan's sister-in-law, upon reading the publicity, approached her local constable on the night of the 26th, and told him that her sister had disappeared and she could not help being nervous that the legs might be hers: she did not want to cause any friction, since she thought that it was up to James himself to go to the police and she did not want to be involved.

It was now too awkward and suspicious for Keenan to stay detached, and on the morning of March 26th, he went to Lanark police station to report his wife as missing from 8.45pm on March 19th – an indication perhaps of time of death. She had said that she was going to London, and she took £50 or £60 with her. This was not quite what he had told her mother. He indicated that he was aware that a woman's legs had been found, but he did not seem unduly perturbed.

Detective Chief Superintendent Muncie interviewed Keenan's sister-in-law, and, hearing about Elizabeth Keenan's ovarian operation, obtained her blood group from the hospital to find out if she could be eliminated from the enquiry, but it was the same as that of the legs. Moving on to interview Keenan at his home, Muncie was unimpressed by him at this first meeting, not liking his furtive glances and the way in which his sullen expression never changed.

Keenan stated that his wife had taken with her a leather shopping bag, which would probably have contained some clothing. The wardrobes were full of women's clothing. He could not say what, if any, items had been taken. One would think that smaller, more intimate articles would have been more telling, but he did not even try to lie in this area, remaining vague and difficult to pin down. Rather than expressing his undying devotion to his wife, as one would have expected, he adopted the hostile pose of only being willing to take Elizabeth back for the child's sake – a clever touch. The policeman's eye noticed that the linoleum beside the bed, which could, conceivably, have borne footprints for purposes of comparison, was exceptionally clean and polished. He took away a pair of shoes. Keenan showed no emotion as he gave his consent. There were no dark blankets to be seen.

James Keenan was Muncie's man – but only to the standard of a hunch. He began to visit the mother-in-law and the sister-in-law frequently, when Keenan was out, having obtained a job as lorry driver's mate, still keeping up his bluff. Elizabeth's mother, frozen with fear and denial, acted strangely: she said at this stage that her daughter had never had any dark blankets in her possession. Muncie thought it most unlikely that £50 to £60 had been available in the house for Elizabeth to take with her. The bookmaker with whom Keenan laid his bets stated that he had been losing for a long time. A relative to whom Keenan owed money had asked him where he had got the money, and, in a corner, he could only say that he had won it on the horses.

Muncie will have known that a woman will only abandon a young child if her life is unbearable, or through mental illness. There was no evidence of either state of affairs. Appeals were made on television nationwide. Keenan cooperated. It appeared that 668 women were missing in the British Isles, and 462 of them were traced as a result of the publicity. Some of them were not pleased. Muncie wondered if Elizabeth could have been involved in an extra-marital relationship. When she worked, she was a flat-bed knitter, a skilled trade, and discreet but negative enquiries were made at her former place of employment.

The street corner near the Keenan's house was a turn-around point for a small, local bus service which left hourly at a quarter to the hour. Was that why Keenan had said that Elizabeth left at 8.45? The driver of the 8.45 bus, however, knew Mrs Keenan and had not seen her at all that evening. Keenan now made a mistake, telling an identifiable lie. Muncie had kept repeating to the family that no one, except James, had heard his wife speak of leaving for London. One morning, Keenan called at a police station and asked the office to pass a message to Muncie that his wife had told his sister that she was thinking of going to London. His sister remembered no such conversation.

Keenan had studiedly not asked about the shoes which had been taken away. The forensic experts were asking for older shoes, more worn. The mother-in-law, who held a key, was taken to the house, and a suitable pair were selected. She was asked to check if any blankets were missing and she said not. The next day, the decision was made to show her the blanket which had been wrapped around the legs, or rather the two quarters of heather-mixture blanket, making up the one half that had been utilised for the legs. She reacted with all the symptoms of shock. 'I know that,' she managed to say, and then 'clammed up'. A doctor was called to her that night, and there was a real feeling that there had been a breakthrough in the case.

Meanwhile, there was an even greater advance when a tinker who had camped near the copse on the prisoner of war site found the torso wrapped in a blanket. It bore the scar of Elizabeth Keenan's ovarian operation, just as Mrs Crippen's remains showed the scar of an operation on the ovaries – in that case for excision. James Keenan was arrested. He had had time to regret using the unusual blankets. Muncie wondered if he had added the detail of the leather shopping bag with some idea of suggesting that his wife might have taken the blankets with her, and then fallen prey to some outside murderer.

It is, of course, in the heat of the moment that mistakes are made. When Mrs Dyer, the baby-farmer, threw an infant into the River Thames at Reading in 1896, one of the sheets of paper in which it was swaddled actually bore her false name and a give-away address. When Dr Buck Ruxton cast the parcelled portions of his wife and maid into a ravine at Moffat, after dismembering them in the bath, his wrapping materials included an identifiable blouse and woollen rompers, and part of the *Sunday Graphic* of September 15th 1935, which was one of a special 'slip' edition sold only in Dr Ruxton's home district, and a copy of which was proved to have been delivered to his house in Lancaster. The brown paper carrier bag in which Keenan had wrapped one of his wife's legs bore a distinctive letter 'A', the mark of an agent for the Household Supply Co, which could, eventually, have led back from a third party to the sister-in-law and thence to Keenan's house.

Because the hands were now available, fingerprinting, with many impressions taken from 40 Wellwood Avenue, was possible at last, but the torso's fingers were withered and at first only seven points of comparison were found, and a minimum of 16 is required for identification. The house was searched. The bath U-bend contents reacted positively to a blood test, as did the panel in front of the bath, almost at floor level. There were no bone particles in any of the U-bends, as had been hoped. Scouring powder had been used vigorously.

The mother-in-law, who had been seen by a doctor, was well enough to state that she had actually given her daughter three heather-mixture blankets as a present after a bedroom fire around Christmas, the traces of which Muncie had observed days previously. She identified the pieces of blanket from the legs and torso, and revealed that she had asked James to leave her house because she could not bear to look at him. At midnight on May 1st, the team achieved a 16 point fingerprint identification.

James Keenan was charged with murder and made no reply. He was searched, and when asked to empty his pockets, he drew out a piece of string to which a shred of material was adhering. Twelve fibres matched fibres from the blanket around the legs and torso. There was also a twist of blue cellulose acetate fibre which matched a shred on the surface of one of the pieces of blanket. The incriminating blankets had a history all of their own: they bore a wartime utility label and had been a present to Elizabeth's mother from a cousin who had worked at the aforementioned prisoner of war camp, and had bought them at the deplenishing sale over 20 years before.

After a night in the police cells, Keenan made a statement in which he confessed to the murder. He told the police where to find the still missing head, which was retrieved from the wood. The features were well preserved. On June 3rd, 1969, he pleaded Guilty at the High Court in Edinburgh and was sentenced to life imprisonment.

CHAPTER 11
RURALITY

The rural idyll has never been the same since Sherlock Holmes' well-remembered words to Watson during a railway journey: 'You look at these scattered houses, and you are impressed by their beauty. I look at them, and the only thought which comes to me is a feeling of their isolation and of the impunity with which crime may be committed there.'

Man's frail homely castle is just an illusion. *I'll huff and I'll puff, and I'll blow your house down.* There are strange undertones to the sudden entry of Father Christmas, *alias* Robin Goodfellow. The hearth was the symbolic and spiritual centre of the home, the abode of the *lares* and *penates*, the household gods. When cottages were low, humped buildings, with a wide primitive chimney which filled the room with smoke when the wind blew hard, that chimney was a possible means of ingress for an intruder, especially frightening if you lived alone with no one to hear your cries. The symbolism of ravishment is only too obvious.

Miss Mary Smith, a quiet woman of 63, lived on her own in a lonely, one-roomed cottage by the wayside at Redhill, in the parish of Auchterless. She was last seen alive and well during the evening of Monday, April 9th, 1849. A fair was being held that day at the village of Badenscoth. It had a reputation for a degree of rowdiness, and although not really worried, Mary had casually remarked to someone that she was not afraid of anybody, 'except that lad, Jamie Robb.' Prophetic words, and truly reported.

James Robb, aged 22, was the Nogood Boyo of the district. He was a stout, strong young man, employed as a labourer at a slate quarry – heavy work. Living at his father's house, near Redhill, he was not some marauding stranger, some casual itinerant, but knew Mary Smith's circumstances, for sure. He would not have slipped down the chimney of a cottage packed with sturdy menfolk to get a light for his pipe without a by-your-leave as he was soon to claim inventively.

On the Tuesday morning, when there was no sign of her moving around outside her home, people who knew her and were in the habit of speaking to her as they passed became concerned. Their behaviour gives the lie to Holmes' jaundiced view of 'these lonely houses, each in its own fields, filled for the most part with poor ignorant folk who know little of the law. Think of the deeds of hellish cruelty, the hidden wickedness which may go on, year in, year out, in such places, and none the wiser.'

They opened the door and went in. Mary Smith was lying dead in her bed, which was broken, with the sheets all crumpled and bearing signs of a terrible struggle. The cause of death was not obvious, and was indeed kept secret for a time but it became known that rape had taken place. There were clues aplenty, and good detective work was not lacking. The chimney was a square wooden box about five feet high by two and a half feet wide, positioned about eight feet above the hearth. The soot was examined: it was partly damp and partly dry and it showed to perfection the streaks such as a man's corded dress would make as he slithered down with foul intent.

An unusual composite metal button bearing words and figures was found, broken from its neck or eye, in a lirk or fold in the sheets. A walking stick had been left outside, by the door, and it was thought that James Robb had had it with him at the fair, 'or one very like to it'. It was easy to assemble a picture of his recent activities. He had left Badenscoth fair at

10.00pm, vowing that he was determined to gratify his passion on somebody before he went to sleep. An acquaintance walked halfway home with him, separating at a point where he would have had to pass Redhill to get to his house that night. The next day, he turned up for work at the quarry at one o'clock. One of his fellow-workmen brushed some soot from his coat and remarked that he must have been in a lum (chimney). There was a button missing from his coat.

George Webster, Sheriff Officer, turfed James Robb out of bed in the middle of the Tuesday night, whereupon he admitted that he had shinned down the chimney, but for the aforementioned innocent purpose. However, the button proved to be an exact match and it fitted the broken eye, with its bright recent fracture, which remained on his coat. When they brought Robb up for trial for murder and 'raptus' in September, 1849, the hearing proceeded behind closed doors. The jury returned a verdict of Guilty, but recommended mercy, because they thought that he had had no intention of committing murder. For the defence, Mr Shand submitted that since the jury had negatived intent to murder, the sentence should not reflect that crime, but he was overruled.

Lord Cockburn was on the bench, and his diary reveals that Robb had a snowball's chance of surviving the flames of his wrath: 'It is difficult to drive the horrors of that scene out of one's imagination. The solitary old woman in the solitary house, the descent through the chimney, the beastly attack, the death struggle – all that was going on within this lonely room amidst silent fields, and under a still, dark sky. It is a fragment of hell which it is both difficult to endure and to quit. Yet a jury, though clear of both crimes, *recommended the brute to mercy*! because he did not *intend* to commit the murder! Neither does the highwayman, who only means to wound, in order to get the purse, but kills.'

The cause of death, as discovered by medical experts, was, according to Cockburn, 'an incipient disease in the heart, which agitation made dangerous but which might have lain long dormant. The violence of the brute, and the alarm, proved fatal.' Mary Smith, 'never married, or a mother' – a polite euphemism – died in the young man's very grip, as he fully confessed after conviction. The cause could also have been anaphylactic shock, or suffocation. One cannot help wondering if he might have killed her anyway, after the attack, since she could identify him. He was hanged by Calcraft on October 16th, 1849, solemnly denying his guilt except as to rape and not understanding the niceties of the law.

James Robb may have been just a rascal who got drunk and went too far, but George Christie, perpetrator of the Kittybrewster tragedy better fits the category of brute, or monster. He was a much older man, to start with, aged 51, and he stood out from his fellows, being six feet tall, and of proportionate muscular power. His features were coarse and sensual and his aspect dogged and sullen. Once he had been in the service of the East India Company, receiving a pension therefrom until he was deprived of its benefits around 1850, after being convicted for robbery of silver plate from Murtle House. Since then, he had had to make shift to earn a shilling where he could.

In October, 1852, he was thrashing corn in a barn belonging to Peter McRobbie, a farmer, or gardener, or both, of Sunnybank Farm, Oldmachar, near Aberdeen. The barn and an adjoining small cottage stood at a distance from the main farm, near the Kittybrewster toll bar. McRobbie had put out the thrashing or threshing of his bear (barley) to a contractor named Humphrey, who was employing two men to help him – James Sayer and George Christie.

The cottage was let by McRobbie to a widow of good report, Mrs Barbara Ross, who had living with her at that time her grandson, five or six-year-old John Louden. She, too, was in need of every mite that she could get, and undertook light agricultural work such as 'cow feeding'. Lately, she had been supplementing her income by providing meals for the bear thrashers. On Saturday, October 2nd, she mentioned to George Christie that she was going to sell two pigs – which represented quite a few shillings. Felonious intent might have germinated at that moment. On the Monday night, after the pigs had been sold, Christie was in Aberdeen. At 8 o'clock, he set out for Kittybrewster, telling an acquaintance in Virginia Street that he was going back for something that he had forgotten.

At 9 o'clock, McRobbie walked over to the barn through dark fields to see how the thrashers had been getting on. The door was locked. He knew that Barbara Ross held the key and he looked in the window of the cottage, where he saw Christie walking about with a lighted candle. What looked like a woman's shape was lying in front of the fireplace. He knocked at the door and the light went out. Christie appeared. There was something agitated in his manner. Moaning sounds came from within.

McRobbie wisely did not challenge the looming giant, but simply asked for the barn key, which he was given. Then he went to fetch a neighbour, William Grant, who lived at Muiryfold, and together they knocked at the door of the cottage. Christie came out again and they asked him to go with them to the barn. They enquired what that groaning was inside the house. 'The boy has a sair belly,' he replied. The two men watched him re-enter the cottage, and very soon afterwards he came out with a bundle under his arm, locked the door, and went off, whistling.

It was now safe to fetch Constable Richardson from Printfield, and he broke the door open and encountered a scene of slaughter. The floor was running with blood and the widow and the boy were lying dead, their bodies fearfully gashed by a bloodied wood-axe which had been left on the table. There were signs of frenzied ransacking. Constable Richardson left several men at the scene and went to inform the Procurator Fiscal, before setting off with Constable Nicol, one of the night patrol, in search of George Christie.

Humphrey had told them where to find him, and at a house in Lower Denburn, there he was, at half past midnight as large as life, sitting with his woman, drinking hard and muddled in mind. They charged him with the crime and he denied it. He was searched, and a purse containing 14s 6d of silver pig money and a gold ring, soon identified as the property of the late Mrs Barbara Ross, were found on his person. Removed to the watch house at Aberdeen for questioning, he remarked ambiguously, 'this should have been done long ago'. Bloodstains were discovered on his shoes, the legs of his trousers, and the wristbands of his shirt. He had pawned or sold articles belonging to the widow as soon as he had reached the town.

In prison, his mien was morose and he continued to say that he was innocent. In court at Edinburgh for trial on December 23rd, 1852, still dark of countenance, he sighed deeply when dreadful matters were adduced, as if he felt something inwardly. His Counsel argued that the real murderer could have left the scene before Christie stumbled upon it and was tempted to steal. The medical evidence, following post-mortem, and based upon body temperature, was that the boy had survived the attack for several hours – that is, he had lain there still alive while Christie, unconcerned, selected the poor widow's valuables.

No doubt, this information influenced the minds of the jury, for they returned a unanimous verdict of Guilty. He was sentenced to be fed only bread and water before his execution at Aberdeen on January 13th, 1853. During his last week on earth he tried to starve himself to death but was dissuaded by doctrinal reasoning. He went bravely, a giant dropping like a tree, and someone had loved him to judge by the banshee wail from a woman in the crowd.

In a confession made to the prison governor, he said that he had been overcome by irresistible rage. He had been, he related, to see Humphrey to collect some outstanding wages, but he had not been at home. Then he had proceeded to the widow's cottage to collect a flagon and a bag which he had left there. She was milking a cow in the byre. She told him that she would not let him have the articles until he had paid her the money which he owed her for milk and food. He flew into a rage and seized the axe. The little boy tried to shield her and got in the way, which further inflamed him. They fled into the cottage, but Christie pursued them, a bellowing monster with an axe, and swung it again and again with all the strength of his long brawny arms. Today, we would test his brain-waves. He was buried in the precincts of the prison, beside the grave of James Robb.

CHAPTER 12
THE NORTHFIELD MYSTERY

The candles lit, it was the hour before supper, and the Laird of Northfield, clad in a nightgown, was sitting in his great chair with his legs crossed jauntily and a pinch of snuff poised between his finger and thumb. He was in good form, almost his usual jocose self, feeling rather better, thank you. Of late, truth to tell, he had been under the weather. The doctor said it was asthma, with a high fever, whatever that meant.

Alexander Keith, who was aged 64, was of that familiar old type – a choleric, hard-riding, hard-drinking landowner, with a large estate in the parish of Gamrie, Banffshire. Just once, he had broken rank by taking a second wife who was right out of his class. Helen Watt was a fisherman's daughter, from the village of Crovie, and family ructions had ensued when he brought her to the big house as his bride, 20 years previously. Relatives refused to speak to the upstart and, in particular, George Keith, the rightful son and heir, the eldest son of the laird's first wife, who had died, had never relented in his animosity. He had left home and set up an establishment in the neighbourhood.

Five children had been born of the new union: in 1756, the second family at Northfield consisted of William (17), Henrietta (15), Elizabeth (13), Alexander (10) and Helen (7). William Keith, the eldest, was his father's favourite – not George, for obvious reasons. Gradually, as Northfield's health had begun to break down – and his drinking habits were blamed – the relationship between husband and wife had become less idyllic. There were frequent spats or 'squabbles'. They were out of temper with each other.

Elspet Bruce, a close family servant, once saw Mrs Keith flying out of the house in a passion, crying to God that she wished her husband had broken his own neck when he broke his horse's neck, and then she 'would not have gotten so much anger by him.' William Taylor of Darfash, loyal retainer of Northfield, heard Mrs Keith say that if God would not take her husband, she wished the devil would: the trouble was that his master liked a dram and Mrs Keith thought that he was extravagant.

Yet he was not an undutiful man, because, being told by his doctors that he had not long to live, and being of the same opinion himself, he had recently executed a valid will to make provision for Helen Keith and her children, in the form of certain charges which the estate could easily support. The main inheritance was, of course, to go to George Keith who was angry and waiting and would have no mercy on the interlopers.

Now, on the evening of November 22nd, 1756, as he sat out of bed and contemplated the affairs of his estate, Northfield felt some remission in his poor health. Perhaps he was not going to die, after all, and the doctors were wrong, as they generally were. Come to think of it, he had not clapped eyes on one of them for eight days. As one finds in these tales, the attending physician was wont to eschew the death-bed if he thought the case was hopeless, and beg not to be sent for again. Northfield's doctor, Mr Chap, surgeon of Old Deer, had taken Helen Keith to one side and told her that her husband was dying: she should not call him back unless he grew better, and meanwhile, here were two blistering plasters to place to the skin.

It had not been a bad day for the ailing laird. There had been some visitors and they had had a good laugh. His friend, the Reverend James Wilson, who had witnessed his will, had come to see him. James Manson, the shoemaker, had shaved him, as usual, that evening. Soon it was suppertime and his wife and all five offspring were with him in his room to encourage him, but he was not very hungry and took only two spoonfuls of slops consisting of aleberry (corn boiled in beer) or kail-brose (the scum of a broth of greens mixed with oatmeal).

Henrietta and Elizabeth went away to their own room and Northfield was now alone with his wife and 17-year-old son, and the two very young children. What exactly happened next comes only from the separate accounts of Helen and William Keith, and they were noted to be consistent. Northfield asked to be helped into bed, and a pair of blankets, freshly warmed, were wrapped around him, since he was complaining of feeling cold. His wife and young Helen and Alexander shared a bed placed at the foot of the big bed. William was, unusually, staying in the room because his father had said something about being afraid that he might die in the night, and Helen wanted him close at hand.

William threw off all his clothes, except his breeches, and prepared to get into his father's bed, to warm his back. He put out the candle and as he leant over the side of the bed, he thought that he could not hear his father breathing. In a panic, he called to his mother to get up at once and light the candle, for his father was either dead or dying, and then he ran to the door and shouted for the two elder girls and the maid, Elspet Bruce, who emerged from her bed in the kitchen, which was divided by a timber partition from the bedroom. She had heard no untoward sounds that evening.

By the light of the candle, while all those present watched, William peered at his father's face and saw that one eye was shut, and the other open. His lips quivered a little, and he was just breathing. William sent the maid out to fetch William Spence, a servant who was drying corn at the kiln, and when they returned, the open eye was half closed, and the breathing ceased. The maid was sent out again, to fetch John and Ann Keith, the laird's brother and sister. According to Elspet Bruce, when she returned with the two kin, Northfield's body had already been taken out of bed and 'streikit upon a deal' (laid out on a board). According to Helen and William Keith, this was not done until the brother and sister had arrived. It was now about 10.00pm.

Next morning, George Keith came storming round to look after his inheritance. It is possible that he had not, until then, heard of the provisions of the will, and he was not pleased. Elspet sent him in to view his father's corpse and the events then became horribly out of the ordinary, with far-reaching consequences. There was a 'blae mark' around the neck. This was new to Elspet and she had a look and she, too, saw the blue mark, about the breadth of two fingers, and also a 'blae spot' on the breast. Whether or not they were misinterpreting *post mortem* signs out of lack of knowledge and distress, or whether these were genuine signs that, as William expressed it to the maid, there had been foul play, is the crux of the Northfield mystery. The widow and William were to offer a practical explanation which was not quite consistent, one to each. There is also the possibility that, out of malice, George was deliberately magnifying an innocent occurrence in order to bring down the hated step-family.

There was ample evidence that the blae marks did exist. William Taylor, the loyal servant, lifted the cloth from his master's face when he was 'streikit' and saw a blue mark on the neck, about the breadth of three fingers, but could not say if it went all round the neck. John Strachan, wright of Gardenstoun, who made the laird's coffin and put in the corpse, stated that young Northfield turned down the grave-clothes and showed him a mark round the forepart of the neck, but he did not see the back. There was a mark reaching down towards the 'slot' of the breast. Both marks were of a blackish blue, like the neck of a fowl newly strangled. James King, Strachan's assistant, saw a black-red mark round the neck, such as he had never seen before on a corpse. Alexander Hepburn, of Cushnie, who was present, saw some blue spots on the breast, and a 'blue girth' that went round the neck, and it was like 'bruised blood'. On the back of the neck he saw a mark 'like what is occasioned by a knot drawn strait'. No one else described a knot mark. No doctor was called to the corpse. There was no procedure for certification of death. It was up to lay people to assess when life had ceased, to hover with feathers and mirrors. No wonder that premature burial was a real fear.

The widow was standing by at the 'chesting', and she heard the mutterings. Hepburn considered that she seemed unwilling to have the corpse inspected, saying that there was nothing unseemly to be seen. She helped to put in the body, and as the coffin was rather 'scrimp' in length, she pressed the head down into it – an unseemly action, one would have thought. Taylor said that no one was actually hindered from looking at the corpse.

He, Taylor, now publicly asked the widow what was the meaning of the blae mark. She replied that it was caused by a string tied around the neck in life 'for holding on a plaister'. William Keith's explanation, given even more publicly, on a later occasion, was that a blistering plaster had been applied to the back, and when it was taken off, kail blades were put to the same place and tied on with the laird's garters, which went below the armpits and round the farther sides of the neck. The feasibility of this weird arrangement was never challenged, so perhaps it was in common use: they must have been long garters, going several times round the leg to secure the breeches. Cabbage leaves are still used in country districts for various inflammatory conditions.

The garters stayed in that position until the grave linen was put on, when William allowed that he did see a blue spot on the left breast, about the breadth of three fingers, but there was nothing that he saw around the neck: the whole body was grossly swollen. So there was a denial of the neck mark seen by others and not denied by William's mother. A 'string' is not the same as an arrangement of garters.

That night in the house of mourning, with its strained atmosphere, George Keith was sitting by the corpse. Mrs Keith asked William what George should have for his supper, whereupon, and William Taylor heard this, William Keith, 17-years-old, hospitably remarked that a 'guid full of the dog's meat was good enough for him: he had no business there, and little hindered him to take a gun to shoot him.'

The time came to discuss the day for the burial. There was a dispute: the widow wanted it on the following Thursday, but George Keith wanted to wait until the Saturday. The Thursday it was. On that day, the Reverend James Wilson was placed in an awkward position. George Keith had taken him upstairs for a private word, to tell him that his father had not got justice in his death. He begged the minister to look at the body and advise him how to act, but Mr Taylor declined, pleading ignorance in such matters and bidding him to consult the medical fraternity. Alone with the responsibility of his suspicions – if they were genuinely based – George objected that he had already written to Mr Finlay, surgeon of Fraserburgh, and had heard in return that he 'could do nothing single' and advised him to seek the assistance of the two physicians at Banff. Nothing more was heard of Mr Finlay, nor did Dr Chap, who had washed his hands and left two plasters, reappear in any guise.

As they were talking in the upstairs room, George Keith and the minister suddenly saw from the window that the corpse, which had been waiting outside the house, had gone without them. It was three to four miles to the graveyard. The young laird left in pursuit of the cortège, on foot, and the minister set off on horseback. George caught up after one and a half miles. Soon afterwards, George wrote a letter to his uncle, James Gordon, of Techmuiry (who was brother to Northfield's first wife) expressing his strong suspicion that his father had been strangled by Helen and William Keith, and asking how to proceed. The uncle advised him not to prosecute unless he had clear evidence. He himself did not attend the funeral, and never had much to do with Northfield after his second marriage, which he considered to have been a disgraceful affair. He did go to his niece's wedding (that was the daughter from the first marriage) but only on condition that Helen Keith was not admitted.

The air was thick with accusation, and those who lived and worked around them were intrigued to note that the widow and her cherished young William were beginning to fall out after the funeral. William told a servant, Janet Watt, that his mother was a liar, a thief, and a murderer. William Taylor, who saw, heard and knew everything, overheard William saying to his mother that if it had been her four quarters, his father might have been living yet. The meaning of 'four quarters' is obscure: it might refer to the portions of the settlement on the estate; or to instalments of her allowance; or, in an old meaning used here to belittle, a quarter was a farthing. His mother would never get justice, William was said to have continued in the same unfilial vein, till she was hung up beside William Wast, and he, William Keith, would be happy to pull on her feet. This ghastly reference was to a felon of the same parish, a ship's captain who had murdered his wife and had been executed in 1752, his body left hanging in chains at Aberdeen for many years.

James Booth, a tailor of Banff, came upon Helen and William Keith quarrelling in his house. The mother said to her son, 'I know as much of you as would get you hanged.' This dreadful state of affairs continued for ten years. The widow and her five children had to vacate the big house in favour of the rightful heir. William Keith grew to manhood, married and had children. He was not living with his mother. At the time of the harvest of 1761, the widow went to William Keith and offered her services as a shearer, but he turned her away, remarking to his shearers that his mother would never get justice till she was hanged.

When he had, at first, been living with his mother, William had been afflicted with 'ghosts and apparitions', like Macbeth. Isobel Robertson, a servant, knew all about it: the young man was trying to sleep in the bed in which his father had died, but was 'troubled' and a lad, James Irvine, was deputed to share the bed with him. There was a rumour that he was afraid of his stepbrother, George.

The Church and the Faculty of Medicine had failed him, but eventually, still in the grip of his obsession, whether or not it was justified, George Keith turned to the law for retribution. He had no new evidence. Certain witnesses who might have supported the widow's side had died. He had marshalled a formidable band of witnesses to buttress his assertions. It was ten years after the event when George Keith laid information and set on the prosecution of his stepmother and stepbrother.

He himself was not allowed to testify at the trial of Helen and William Keith on July 13th, 1766, because it was argued that he had acted as an agent, attended the precognition, and directed the questions to be put to the witnesses. The proceedings were remarkable in so many ways. The defence objected that the judge had left the court on one occasion, so that anyone could have approached the jury, but it turned out that he had only retired to a corner for the benefit of a little fresh air. A member of the jury, William Forbes of Skellater, found himself in deep trouble for absconding and being seen making for the New Inn, but he had, he claimed, gone out on a necessary occasion.

The long and singular indictment charged that after the execution of the will, the prisoners became impatient for

Northfield's death in order to obtain the benefits, but as counsel for the two Keiths pointed out, they were in fact better off before the death of the laird, following which the heir came into his inheritance. Furthermore, it did not make sense that they should 'wantonly imbrue their hands in the blood of a husband and a father, merely to obtain a few days, perhaps a few hours, earlier possession of the moderate allowance which he had left them.'

What was really needed was medical evidence as to the condition of Northfield's body both before and after death, but, as we have seen, none was available. The only medical evidence came from Dr Alexander Irvine, of Banff, who stated that the blue marks, as described, could not, in his experience, have been caused by any disease in the absence of external violence. Counsel for the defence, however, well argued that the jury should bear in mind 'how various the appearances of dead bodies often are', and that the marks were spoken of by 'ignorant country people' remembering events that had taken place ten years previously.

The indictment, incidentally, charged that 'there had been no such plaister or dressing tied on with garters upon the deceased that evening' but no evidence to support that important contention, framed in the mind of George Keith, has survived. Years afterwards, it began to be suggested that the blue marks were, in fact, hypostatic lividity, which theory might be supported by the vivid words of the coffin-maker, John Strachan, to the effect that the marks were of a blackish blue, like the neck of a fowl newly strangled. Such changes begin to develop an hour or two after death.

The jury, however, convicted both parties by a majority of nine to six, for what was the future science of forensic pathology to William Forbes of Skellater (even though that gentleman was, as it happens, of the precedent family of Dr Forbes Winslow, famous Victorian alienist)? Quite soon, Helen and William Watt were granted a free pardon, but William died within a few weeks from an unknown cause. The mother lived on into obscurity. Their behaviour certainly had been suspicious, but, as recorded, it arose only after George Keith had seen and possibly misinterpreted the condition of the body.

There was no feasibly discernible motive for murder. Why kill a dying man when euthanasia is not an issue? Why kill and render your own position in life less comfortable? They knew that would be the result. There were no great expectations. If murder it was, could it have arisen out of a sudden access of hatred and revulsion? Helen Keith had complained about her husband's temper. Romantic love had fled. Perhaps he enjoyed reminding her about her humble origins. She was tired. It was late. There were two young children. She was going to be ousted from her home. It was not fair. She was expected to nurse an invalid who was described as valetudinarian. It was all getting on her nerves. We are told that he had 'purged' in the room after spooning up his meal of slops, which he then imagined that he had instantly eliminated. He was in her power. Did he say something not piteous but taunting, and did she then fall upon him in front of young William's horrified eyes, and did his already weak and failing heart then give out after even a modicum of violence?

CHAPTER 13
BLUE VITRIOL

James Humphrey was a butcher, who also kept a public house in a poor part of Aberdeen. Catherine, his wife, was a scold, a virago, and the excess of matrimonial drinking made worse the war between them. Everyone knew that Kate hated her husband. She was a shrew, constantly threatening to kill him. Once she had rhetorically asked someone to fetch her some laudanum, to finish him off. There was a wretched, scuttling servant who saw her with a knife clutched in her bony hand, making play to cut Master's throat. An innocent bystander was treated to the sight of a melodramatic tableau: Humphrey was exposing his neck and inviting his wife to use the long razor in her hand. 'There,' he said, 'do it now, for you will do it some time.' Both parties had a picturesque turn of phrase. He said that she would swing for him yet, with her face looking down Marischal Street after him.

On the night of Friday, April 16th, 1830, there was an explosive quarrel and clash of wills in the house. Blows were exchanged. Catherine had allowed in a woman who was supposed to have tried to poison her husband, and James, disapproving, had forcibly evicted her. Kate was annoyed. She sent her servant to bed before her, which was unheard of. The girl heard her imprecation – 'Lord God, if anybody would give him poison, and keep my hand clear of it!' The servant slept. James slept in the kitchen with his mouth open, as always. Kate lay in the room opposite. The servant woke. Mistress was there 'on her stocking soles' telling her to get up because James was taken ill and making a noise. Mistress smiled as she imparted this information.

The servant went down and found James Humphrey writhing in agony and roaring out, 'I'm burned – I'm gone – I'm roasted!' 'You must have taken bad drink,' Kate kept suggesting. 'Oh! Woman, woman, whatever I have gotten, it was in my own house.' There were burn marks on the bedclothes. Several people had come in to help. A child put its lips to a glass that was standing on the table, and cried out that it had been burnt. The servant noticed that there were three glasses where only two had been when Master retired for the night. The clues were strewn as thick as leaves: a phial of oil of vitriol (sulphuric acid), kept by the window, which, the day before, had contained three or four teaspoons of the stuff, kept in those days to use in solution as a 'tonic' and so on, was now nearly empty.

A doctor was called, but he was tending a dying man. Kate remarked *sotto voce* to her servant, 'Take care of my keys, come of the *** what like.' A neighbour bent over the sufferer and asked him what ailed him. 'Bad work, bad work,' was the reply. 'May God Almighty forgive them who have done this to me.' Over and over again he insisted that he had got no drink but from his own Kate, and never mentioned his spluttering, burning awakening. Kate at his bedside was seen to be wringing her hands and kissing him. The Reverend Mr Hart was in attendance, and he earnestly enquired if Humphrey had any suspicion of his wife. 'No, no,' said James, steadfast to the end, and so he died, on Sunday morning.

Catherine Humphrey was brought up at the Autumn Circuit, and her dignity and decent appearance were remarked upon, but the jury voted to a man for Guilty. A few days after capital sentence had been passed upon her, she made a full confession, admitting that she had poured the oil of vitriol down her husband's throat as he slept. In such a way did the ghost of Hamlet's father complain, 'Sleeping within my orchard/ My custom always of the afternoon,/ Upon my secure hour thy uncle stole,/ With juice of cursed hebona in a vial,/ And in the porches of my ears did pour/ The leperous distilment.'

Jealousy and malice, Kate Humphrey said, had led her to commit the cruel crime. An immense crowd came to witness the hanging of the woman in black. She did not raise her eyes to glimpse the human race that she was leaving. But she dropped her handkerchief as a signal to the executioner that she was ready and was heard to say quietly 'Oh! My God!' She struggled a little on the rope, and twice raised her hands.

The grounds for Mrs Humphrey's expressed jealousy were not revealed, but vitriol is, of course, traditionally the remedy of choice for a woman scorned – topically, in the face, or internally, if she can find a way. Anne Inglis was another dangerous fury, and she, too, gave ample advance warning of her intent. These murders from sexual jealousy were premeditated but not kept secret, rather broadcast to the whole world. Patrick Pirie was the betrayer who died for his fault. Anne was his servant at Malheurust (an unhappy name) in the parish of Alva. He was a bachelor of 32 when he took her to bed, with sweet promises, but then he began to court another, and marriage was spoken of, whereupon Anne Inglis vowed revenge. There would be a burial before there was a bridal, was how she put it. The funeral bak'd meats would coldly furnish forth the marriage tables! In the spring of 1795, shortly before the proposed marriage, Patrick Pirie was laid low with vomiting and severe pains all over his body, but he was a strong man and within a fortnight was on his feet again. That was when he accepted a draught of ale from the hand of Anne Inglis. After nine days of agony – vomiting, pains, great heat in the stomach and swelling in the extremities – he died, blaming his servant, Anne. The body was opened and terrible inflammation of the stomach was observed: the inner coat was corroded and actually separated from the contiguous lining.

The physicians did look for arsenic, but there was no trace.

On the day after the autopsy, a search was made of a chest belonging to Anne Inglis and, lo and behold! blatantly within, when it could have been removed, was a paper parcel of blue vitriol. She bleated that it was for the toothache, although this was the first that anyone had heard of it. It was remembered that on the day before her master's death she had been seen with some teacups whose rims were smeared with a bluish powder. One of the cups contained something that looked like quicksilver. Could this mean that she had added mercury to the vitriol? Again, we have overt signals of what she had been at, and by now we might be thinking that Anne Inglis was a little simple, but the unexpected resolution of this tale is that the jury acquitted her.

The medical evidence had been that if blue vitriol had been administered, no trace of it would have been found in the stomach, due to the medicines prescribed, and the evacuations. It was thought that the jury might have been influenced by the doctors' further comment that, unless they had been told of the suspicion, they would not have concluded that this was a death by poison, since there were no external appearances to support the proposition.

Blue vitriol is copper sulphate, powerfully corrosive salts with a pronounced metallic taste. In 1886, a man named Reynolds tried to kill his wife with blue vitriol in spruce and peppermint water. (The green tops of spruce-tree were mixed with a solution of sugar or treacle.) In 1884, a servant-girl, Mary Baker, poisoned her mistress with copper sulphate in a jug of beer, but failed to kill, because the taste was soon noticed. One ounce is given as the fatal dose. Its main domestic use seems to have been as a greener of vegetables (a bad idea) but not as a cure for toothache. The vomited matters should have been blue in Patrick Pirie's case, but no doubt there was no expert standing by to analyse them.

CHAPTER 14
THE BATTERED BRIDE

John Adam stands out somewhat from our other sinners lapped in the flames of the everlasting bonfire. But for constitutional stirrings of lust, avarice and sloth, he could have taken the yellow brick road to fulfilment, instead of the primrose way to the high lonely gallows-tree beside the Moray Firth.

Although not of a confessing disposition, his eyes dazzled, and he covered them, when he saw what he had done. The old Adam was locked into his soul, and began to emerge when he was only 14 years of age. He was a thinker, and, in small measure, a leader, but the contemplation of man's place in the world and in society led him into dissatisfaction with his low station in life. His physical presence was strong, compelling, and he had power over women. Not to put too fine a point on it, he was a womaniser, a fleet-footed seducer. Maidens and widows, all fell beneath his flails. Prevarications – plain lies and damned lies – tripped from his tongue, but when he was a stripling he was valued for the wondrous tales he told.

Born all fresh on New Year's Day in 1804, from crofters' stock, he was the son of an elder of the Kirk, whose righteousness proved to be an impossible model. The father died when John Adam was 14, and that was when the lurking faults in his character began to influence the pattern of his life. He was handsome and obliging, but popularity had done him no good. Now it was his turn to manage the old 20-acre farm of Craigieloch, Lintrathen, near Forfar, of which his ancestors had been tenants for 300 years. His widowed mother turned to him to step into his father's shoes, but, in suggestive words, 'he proved unequal to the duty', a disappointment, and was sent away to work on another farmstead. There he grew up, and returned to his rightful place after five years of exile, with his tendency to idleness and disregard for the truth well noted.

At the age of 20, he was admitted a member of the Kirk and sat in his father's pew, a regular and devout communicant. There is no reason to doubt the sincerity of his faith, but his private behaviour did not match up to his public face. His fields became neglected, weeds spouted, while he gadded about, sightseeing, or rather visiting the ladies in whom he had now developed a consuming interest. They had no resistance, and misunderstood his attentions. Within a bare two months of his formal reception into the Church of Scotland, there was a resounding scandal, when he was convicted before the Kirk Session of the seduction of two young women of the parish. In each case, the father was an elder, and great was the repulsion felt, because one girl, who was deaf and dumb, was his own cousin. His company was no longer sought, and he was forced to move away.

John Adam had strayed from the path and was henceforth a restless wanderer, discontented, pursued for vengeance. Agricultural labouring was all that he had to offer, and he found employment at Carrisbank Farm, near Brechin, no more than 20 miles distant, where he was attracted to a young woman named Jane Brechin [sic]. Unusually, she saw through him, and, perceiving that he did not intend marriage, turned him down. Stung by this unwonted rejection, he walked out, taking a similar job near Aberdeen. Jane Brechin had made a mortal mistake.

Aberdeen widened Adam's horizons, and he got in with a group of freethinkers who were drawn to Deism – that movement which evinced a strong aversion from Christianity, and held the belief that the lights of nature and reason are sufficient guides. Adam himself purchased a copy of Tom Paine's *Age of Reason* from a chapman at a fair in Aberdeen, and it became, as it were, the textbook of his set. Enraptured by Paine's crude and homely logic, his fiery Republicanism, and criticisms of the Bible, Adam abandoned his strong grounding in the Kirk.

This group of his was, in some ways, wild and loose, but he stood apart, not abandoned to the fleshpots, preferring to seduce the respectable class of women. Soon Aberdeen could hold him no more. His philandering had become notorious, and he had to flee to Lanarkshire. At last, for the first time in his life, he felt true love for a girl, and proposed marriage. The date was set and he intended to be at the altar. I hope that this part of his history is correct, but I suspect that it is his own voice that can be heard, inventing retrospectively.

The story of John Adam is punctuated by luminous set pieces, tableaux of the imagination. His talent for oneiric narrative was quite remarkable. In anticipation of the wedding, he later said, for effect and sympathy, he had a precognitive dream: at the hour of midnight, his betrothed appeared at his bedside, blanched and beshrouded as for the grave. 'John,' she prophesied, 'we shall never be married, but, mark, you will die an awful death.' In terror he awoke, and in dread he lived through the hours of the day, until it was after noon, and he obtained permission to go to see his affianced. Long miles he walked to her father's house, and arrived with the darkness. As he approached, he heard the sound of psalm singing from within, and, through a chink in the shutters, he saw that the room was draped in white. Friends and neighbours were singing around the bed on which there lay the corpse of his intended bride. She had died suddenly that morning.

Recovered from the shock, and his brush with the supernatural, he dallied elsewhere in compensation, until, in

1831, he was compelled to escape to Glasgow, where he enlisted in the 2nd Dragoon Guards, quartered in the city. He looked very fetching in his uniform, and no woman was safe from his charms. By now he had sunk so low as to rob enamoured widows of their savings.

In the winter of 1833-4, he was with his regiment at Warkworth, in Northumberland, and encountered Dorothy Elliot, the 18-year-old daughter of a well-off innkeeper. From the evidence available, this, in fact, was the one for whom he felt a constant love, but since his time was running out, who can tell how long those tender feelings would have lasted. Back in Scotland in March, 1834, he deserted from his regiment and made his way down to Warkworth to persuade Dorothy to elope with him. Overcome with the romance of his approach, she agreed, on condition that there would be a marriage ceremony at the end of the first stage.

However, John Adam was too flighty a bird to be netted, and by ruse and excuse, lie and procrastination, he put her off and bore her home triumphantly to meet his relatives at Lintrathen, where she passed as his newly-wed, and all rejoiced. After an enjoyable visit, the happy pair left for Inverness by various ambages, in order to avoid the military authorities. Adam experienced some difficulty in cashing a purse of English banknotes, which were, alas! the proceeds of robbery, but he prevailed, and the couple went on to Dingwall, and lived as Mr and Mrs John Anderson. Adam delved in the local quarries, and there was domestic bliss until the autumn of 1834. Dorothy was pregnant, the English money was spent, the quarry work was too hard, and underpaid, and it was time for a variation in their circumstances.

Judged by his previous form, Adam would have summarily abandoned his responsibilities, but, surprisingly, he schemed to keep his family together, although the method that he came up with was as wicked as could be. Telling Dorothy that he had to visit an aged aunt from whom he had great expectations, he set forth. Dorothy had not heard of such a benefactrix, but she had found her quasi-husband ever bad at communication, and she raised no objection. He was not, anyway, a man whom you would lightly cross. His mission was to seek out Jane Brechin, the woman who had spurned him. He had heard that she had done well for herself and was in a good way of business in Montrose.

Dressed in his best bib and tucker he materialized in Jane's thriving little shop and presented himself as a lost suitor from the misty past who had long pined for her romantically and regretted his former *bêtises*. Not married, older, she was flattered, and this time she gave in, especially when he asked her to marry him. She was to join him at his house near Inverness. The wedding was set for March 11th, 1835, after due proclamation in church, at her mother's house in Laurencekirk.

Adam helped her to sell up the shop and lodge the proceeds in the bank. It was a small fortune. Then he left and laboured in the quarries of Dingwall, until the date came near, when his presence was again required at the side of his invalid aunt. The Reverend John Cook, parish minister of Laurencekirk, conducted a valid marriage ceremony, although perhaps it might have been voidable later if the bride had survived, *if* the Kirk had such provisions. John Adam was caught at last, but it did not really count, because he was working through the grades of a master plan which would leave him a widower very, very soon.

The couple left by the afternoon coach for the north. The honeymoon night was spent in Aberdeen, then on to Inverness, where Adam installed his bride in respectable lodgings with Hugh and Janet McIntosh at Chapel Street. They were kind people and could not help noticing that during the next few weeks, Mr Adam never spent a full night there, so pressing were his business concerns elsewhere. He kept turning up back in Dingwall, shining with good news: the aunt had died, leaving him all her furniture and a legacy of £100 or so, which he proceeded to place on deposit in the National Bank under the name of John Anderson.

At last the Montrose carrier arrived at Chapel Street with Jane's furniture, which was supposed to improve the messuage at the matrimonial home in waiting, but she was downcast when Adam abandoned her once again, insisting on going on before her with the chattels to make all shipshape for her reception. His true destination, of course, was Dingwall, where Dorothy was overjoyed to receive the aunt's heirlooms – a chest of drawers, a tent-bed, and a trunk. John Urquhart, a sawyer, and his wife, Christina, with whom the 'Andersons' lodged, witnessed the coming of the aunt's worldly goods, and were also rather baffled by John's variant excuses for his absences – visiting a brother or collecting monies left to him by an uncle in India.

There John Adam could have left his fraud and he debated his options within himself. It was noticed that he paid unco' heed to the sermon as he sat in his usual pew in the parish kirk of Dingwall on Sunday, March 29th.

On Monday, the 30th, he was dining with his wife at the lodgings in Inverness. Her new home was ready, he told her. She heard the tidings with great joy, and packed a small basket of personal effects, including a pair of stockings which she was proudly knitting for her husband. Her whole luggage consisted of this basket, some clothing in a bundle, and an umbrella. The McIntoshes had grown fond of the often abandoned bride, and quite possibly suspicious of the comings and goings. They demurred when Adam delayed the journey until the evening, saying that it was too late to set off, but Adam said that they were going only a few miles beyond the ferry after a short stage. They could surely not get further than Redcastle that night, Hugh McIntosh persisted, but Adam said shortly that they might.

It was dusk when the couple left the coach and boarded the

ferry at Kessock. Roderick McGregor, the boatman, conveyed
them across the Stygian waters to the north side of the Beauly
Firth: they sat together in the stern, and by the light of the
boat lamp he recognized the man from a previous occasion
when he had been travelling with some furniture. John Adam
sloped ashore, taciturn as ever, but his wife sweetly bade the
ferryman goodbye, before she followed in her husband's
tracks, all trusting, down the way to Dingwall, across the
lonely promontory of the Black Isle.

It was 10 o'clock that night when Adam returned to his
lodgings at Dingwall. The family had gone to bed and left the
door unlocked for him. He seemed tired, as well he might after
engaging in some strenuous physical activity and tramping
some 12 miles over moorland by moonlight. He brought with
him a basket, a bundle, and an umbrella which he represented
as the last relics of his aunt. It was slightly awkward that, as
Dorothy found when she examined them, the body linen was
marked JB, and one nightdress had not been washed since last
usage, but Adam was quick to devise some explanation. More
difficult, but not insuperable, to account for were the half-
knitted hose with the wires still in them.

The next day, Adam resumed his work in the quarries,
after mentioning to Dorothy that he was thinking that they
might emigrate to America very shortly. Days passed, and
then on Friday, April 10th, John Adam's battered bride, her
life snuffed out, pitiful to behold, was discovered on the moor
of Mulbuie. Three Highland lasses, who could speak only
Gaelic, Jane and Peggy Stewart and Betty Gray, with a lad
named John Campbell, had been planting out fir-trees on the
Braes of Kilcoy. In the evening, Jane and John went to rest in
a roofless cottage beside a disused peat-road. The walls were
partly tumbledown, and the girl noticed a piece of gauze
veiling which was sticking out of the rubble. John told her not
to touch it: some poor person must have thrown it away.
However, when they looked around, they saw a woman's shoe,

embedded in soil. They began to dig with the spades which they had with them, and realized that there was a woman's body buried underneath the stones and soil.

William Forbes, a cottar (cottager) was summoned from his home at Muckernich of Kilcoy, and the clothed body was uncovered. A great stone was seen to be lying flat on the face. The Procurator Fiscal and surgeons from Dingwall were called out to the ruined cottage, and, after preliminary examination, the body was taken to the Town House at Dingwall. John Jones, surgeon, had noted that the dead woman had lain in a corner, and the mass of débris – turf, stones and sand – appeared to be part of the wall, which had been pushed down for the purpose of concealment. In view of the strength of the standing walls, it could not have fallen by accident.

At post-mortem, a heap of clotted blood was found under the head, and the jawbone was fractured at both sides of the head. The tongue protruded an inch out of the mouth and blood issued from the nose. On the scalp were two lacerated wounds which corresponded in size and shape with stones found near the corpse.

No identification was possible as yet; the dead woman appeared to be a stranger to the district. Handbills did the trick: they were distributed widely, bearing the description of a woman aged about 40, clad in a purple stuff gown, with a black silk bonnet and veil. She was wearing a new wedding ring, her linen was marked JB, and there was a pillbox in her pocket, labelled J. Mackenzie, Chemist and Druggist, Forres. (Did the coach pass through Forres on the way to Inverness from Montrose, and did she feel ill on the long journey?)

When John Adam was home from the quarry that night, his wife was full of the news of the mysterious woman in purple. 'They say it is the body of a married woman, John,' she told him in all her innocence, 'for there is a ring on her finger such as married women wear. From her dress of home-made stuff, they think that she must be the wife of some Highland shepherd. How I feel for her husband, poor man, when he hears of her mangled state.' Adam showed no reaction and dourly went about his affairs, removing his £100 deposit from the bank and arranging the emigration details. But he was too late, because reports of the gruesome murder spread across the counties, and, especially in Inverness, the oft-deserted bride with the new wedding ring, who had been wafted away at even, was very well remembered.

On the Sunday, after midnight, officers arrested John Adam in his bed for the murder of Jane Brechin, his lawful wife. Poor, pregnant Dorothy, his wife in all but formality, who had hoped for marriage, was astonished by the revelations and was left behind with the Urquharts to comfort her while Adam was harried in handcuffs to the Town House. Once there, he was deliberately confronted with a ghastly spectacle, which strangely echoed his previous supernatural dream: 'Attendants with their candles stood round the table on which lay the silent figure of the murdered woman, still in her marriage dress, while her comely features bore the marks of brutal violence.'

Waiting grimly for the sinner were various persons from Inverness and they identified both the dead and living. He denied everything. The candles guttered, the gloom of the death-chamber was overwhelming, and one of the women fainted to the floor. John Adam faltered, too: in a brief moment of weakness, he put his hands over his eyes. 'I am not accustomed to such sights,' he apologised to the Procurator Fiscal.

The Fiscal now proceeded upon a 'trial by touch' – that centuries-old ordeal perhaps unexpected in the Age of Reason, or rather a modified form of the rite. If Adam were indeed the murderer, the body should have bled or spoken in tongues, or he should have collapsed or confessed, or some such portent. 'Take that hand in your own, and say if you know it,'

Cameron the Fiscal ordered Adam, and, undaunted, he took in his own the clammy hand of the dead woman, and said that he did not know it. 'Lay your hand on that face, then, and say if you ever saw it before. Then place your hand on that bosom and say if your hand was ever there before.' Boldly Adam placed his hand as directed, and swore, 'I have never seen this woman before, either alive or dead.' 'Very well,' said the Fiscal, 'we are all in the presence of God.'

As if this confrontation were not drama enough, when they removed Adam to the prison at Inverness to await trial, they took him by the scenic route across the moor of Mulbuie, calculated to pass the very scene of the murder, but if they hoped that he would break down and confess, they were sadly disappointed, because he refused to look at the crumbling cottage, and the mournful file continued along the track in the lea of the fir plantation to doom.

The trial of John Adam took place at Inverness on the one day of September 18th, 1835. He was not wearing his usual wig, in order, no doubt, to thwart identification in court and sow doubt, and it was seen that the strikingly handsome man, tall and dark, was, in fact, as bald as a slug, with side-whiskers in compensation for the superior deficiency. He looked older than his years, which was perhaps not such a good idea, making him more menacing.

The alarming indictment charged that he did with a stone or other hard instrument strike his wife two or more violent blows on the head, whereby she was severely wounded and was stunned, and did then violently strike or dash down upon the side of her head a large stone, whereby the jawbone on both sides of her head was fractured, whereof she immediately died; or that she was suffocated by pressure after the assault by means of throwing down upon her part of an old wall, consisting of turf and stones and other materials, and covering her person therewith.

Two large stones, bloodstained, brought on a cart from the

scene of the crime backed up the indictment chillingly. John Adam, as expected, pleaded Not Guilty and lodged special defences: alibi – that he was at the quarry at the relevant time; his good character; prejudice by publication of untrue, improper and cruel statements in the press. John Jones, the surgeon, identified the two stones. One had been found beneath the head. The other, weighing 28lbs, had lain above the head, and its corners corresponded to the bi-lateral fractures of the jaw. The image of John Adam, tall and used to weights, with the massive stone uplifted in his arms, biblical fashion, made a powerful impression in court.

Cross-examination brought up a difficulty in the medical evidence, which was just about Adam's only hope, except that other evidence against him was overwhelming: Mr Jones admitted that his first impression was that of a person very recently dead – up to some two or three days previously. The body seemed quite fresh, with blood flowing from the nose, but the way in which it was covered, and the atmosphere excluded, would go far to retard putrefaction. Obviously, Adam wanted the time of death to be set as long as possible after he had been seen vanishing into the dusk with Jane on March 30th.

Mrs Margaret Munro, of Mill Street, Montrose, a cousin of Jane Brechin, identified John Adam as *the very man*. Jane's basket and umbrella, and the half-knitted stockings (finished by pregnant Dorothy), had been retrieved from Adam's lodgings at Dingwall and brought to court as exhibits: these were eagerly identified by those who had known her. Mrs Janet McIntosh remembered a significant conversation: Jane had told her that her husband was providing her with a comfortable home somewhere between Dingwall and Beauly. She herself had speculated that it must be at Maryburgh, since there was no other place so situated, but Jane said that was not the right name. Of course, for her destination was a ruined cottage with no name in the middle of nowhere.

The evidence as to the manner in which Adam had abstracted Jane's life savings, having obtained her signature, was particularly damning, even if the agent of the British Linen Company's bank at Montrose was totally unable to identify Adam without his wig as the very man who had withdrawn £96 from Jane's account. The defendant's two declarations, read, made a poor impression. The first, dated two days after arrest, was a cobweb of lies: he was verily John Anderson, of Dalkeith, legally married to Dorothy Elliot, and Jane Bunton, his spinster aunt, had bequeathed to him her choice effects. (He was thinking of the tell-tale initials on the linen.)

On May 7th, there had been some considered modifications. He did admit to knowing Jane Brechin and visiting her at Montrose, but it was to demand repayment of certain sums which he had lent to her. She had refused to refund the cash on any consideration except marriage. That was precisely why he had married her, and visited her occasionally at her lodgings in Inverness. She had signed the money over to him. On March 30th, she had taken him aside and told him that she wanted to vacate the lodgings immediately, because they were too cold, and she left with him that evening, with her basket, bundle and umbrella. When they arrived at the Windmill, near the ferry, he observed that the boat was about to start, and hurriedly separated from Jane – he hastening down to the ferry, to get back to Dingwall, and she returning to the town, presumably in search of new lodgings. Since then, he had never seen Jane Brechin, and, as a matter of fact, he was not by any means convinced that the corpse shown to him was that of his wife, since the features were so altered and destroyed. This was all a brave and despicable try, but of course it was at variance with the proven facts.

For the defence, Counsel submitted that the possibility that the woman had been killed accidentally by the falling of the wall had not been excluded, and the prisoner was entitled to the benefit of the doubt. The medical men could not swear that the injuries had been inflicted during life. There was an argument that Adam had deceived Jane Brechin and then merely deserted her. It was not proved that the woman seen with him on the ferry was his wife. It was an ingenious speech, greeted with applause, but the verdict, and it was unanimous, was Guilty.

Adam listened quietly as the judge sentenced him to death, and then cried out, in a loud, pulpit voice, 'You have condemned an innocent man! I am condemned at the bar of man, but I will not be condemned at the bar of God!' The effect was electrifying, and then suddenly he struggled violently with the warders and a hidden razor fell to the ground. In the condemned cell, still posing as an innocent, he asked for the ministrations of the Reverend Alexander Clark, who declared that, personally, he had no doubt but that he was addressing a murderer of the deepest dye. It was thought at the time that Adam saw no advantage in confessing, because he secretly had no belief in an afterlife, and also imagined that an admission of guilt would chain him absolutely to the gallows. They watched him night and day for a suicide attempt, and he complained that the lighted candles disturbed his rest.

Two days before the end, he wrote to the only woman he had cared for – Dorothy Elliot. The letter was said to have been inscribed in his own blood, but, supervised as he was, that seems unlikely. Dorothy, all tears, was allowed to visit him in his gloomy cell, the night before execution. 'Oh, tell her to beware of bad company!' he charged the clerical posse as they led her away.

On Friday, October 16th, 1835, John Adam was taken to the Longman's Grave, beside the Moray Firth, decked out in the obligatory long black camlet robe. When he reached the scaffold and stood upon the drop, he found himself gazing across the bright and glittering waters of the Firth to the far ridge of Mulbuie. He at once turned round and stood with his back to the sea and his face to the people as the executioner approached and did his job.

A deep grave was hewn out beneath the pavings of the old Inverness jail, and he was lowered into it in a standing position. Thus, too, most curiously, was Ben Jonson buried in 1637, with his coffin upright, although in his case it was at his own request, in order, it was said, to extract the promise from King Charles the First of a place in Westminster Abbey.

John Adam confided to an admiring prison crony, for posthumous onward circulation, a confession and a last ghostly revelation, worthy of M R James. He had, he admitted, first sought to suffocate his bride, commando-style, by pressing his thumbs below her ears. 'What do you mean, John? Oh, dear me!' she had protested. Afterwards, fleeing along the high road to Dingwall, by the alternating light of the moon as it slid in and out of the clouds, he beheld a figure coming towards him, and he jumped over a wall and hid. But then, when he went back to the road, he saw the same figure still advancing, and as he walked forward it kept always at a like distance from him. He took to his heels and made for Maryburgh, preceded by his shadow. Afraid to enter the village, he sat down by the roadside and lit his pipe, to steady his nerves, whereupon the phantom of the moors vanished.

CHAPTER 15
THE BABES IN
THE QUARRY

There is something awesome about laked quarries, that makes us draw back from the lip of the bank. I know of a place, an abyss, where dark slopes of granite, hewn out in flakes and harbouring sparse purple weeds, fall sheer, straight into a black tarn of unguessable depth, horribly clouded with swaying, brown algae. In a nightmare, thick eels might lie along sunken ledges, as they are said to do in Loch Ness. Denton Welch, the '40s writer, could have had such a loathsome cauldron in mind when he wrote in his diary of 'ponds dark as molasses treacle where the antlered branches are covered with hair-fungus-moss'. Elliott O'Donnell, author of frightening books on the supernatural, would choose a sunless man-made lake as the setting in which a box-headed elemental spirit might rear up from its den behind a rock and stilt ever forward, with its set yellow eyes aglimmer.

Hopetoun Quarry was deep and dangerous, 1000 yards long, with a curve, and 40 yards wide. The only access was by a winding cartroad, and it was so overhung by trees that you came upon the lonely mere suddenly, and with a shock. It was said no bird sang there, but you don't have to believe that. In the year of 1913, on a hot Sabbath morning in June, two countrymen stopped to rest in the shade of the bending trees by the quarry. They were off the beaten track because Tam Duncan, a ploughman, was showing the new grieve, John Thomson, around the boundaries of Riddrie Mains, a farm, which lay near the village of Winchburgh in West Lothian, 12 miles west of Edinburgh

A bundle was floating on the turgid waters where insects buzzed and hummed. It looked like pieces of wood, or perhaps an old scarecrow. There was something human about the shape, something not quite right. Using a broken branch as a grapple, they dragged the lumpish mass as far as the bank. Then they could see that the object was, in fact, two small bodies, tied together with a length of window-cord, which broke when they tried to lift them out of the water. The police were called, and the local police surgeon, Dr Cross, who must have been behind the times, because he considered that a post-mortem would be a useless procedure, since the bodies had obviously been in the lake for a long period.

Unconvinced, the Procurator Fiscal ordered the remains to be taken to the mortuary at Linlithgow, where Professor Harvey Littlejohn and a young Dr Sidney Smith soon demonstrated the value of forensic science. Their major findings fall under the headings of clothing, sex, age, and contents of stomach, and they led to rapid identification. The bodies were dressed identically in poor quality garments which were nearly rotten: shirts, stockings with garters under the knees, and boots. Breeches were not mentioned but were presumably present. A very substantial clue as to identity was provided by a faded, nearly invisible mark on one of the shirts – the stamp of a poorhouse (workhouse) at Dysart, in Fife.

Gender was not immediately obvious, and investigation of internal glandular structure was necessary to define that both bodies were male. The heights, by direct measurement, were three feet seven and a half inches, and three feet two inches. These were the average heights of a boy of six to seven years, and one of four years. The condition of the teeth confirmed the estimate. The smaller boy still had all his milk teeth. The brown hair of both boys had been cut shortly before death.

The case was unusual because of the extreme degree to which the transformation to adipocere had progressed by reason of long immersion in water, estimated as between 18 months and two years. As a result, the internal organs were remarkably well-preserved and yielded another evidential find. The stomachs were intact, and the contents largely undigested. The boys' last meal had been Scotch broth. Barley, potatoes, whole green peas, turnips and leeks were present, and had been consumed about one hour before death, which suggested that the boys had lived locally or at least had not been brought from a distance to be disposed of at the quarry.

It was not possible to discover the cause of death. There was a small injury in the scalp of the elder boy, with no evidence of fracture nor of whether it had been inflicted before or after death. There was no doubt, from the circumstances, that a double murder was committed, but, so terrible was the crime, that there seems to have been a taboo attached to speculation about the method of killing. I shall respect those scruples, except to comment that one of several variables is indeed too frightful to contemplate.

From the start, the pathologists thought that the boys had walked willingly along that winding track to their deaths, in the company of someone they knew. The most obvious suspect to search for had to be some poor, crazed woman unable to cope with her family, deluded perhaps, and the crime was also uncomfortably reminiscent of the deeds of the Victorian baby-farmers. There was never any discussion in those perhaps more innocent times that the murders were sexually motivated.

The pathologists were more concerned to assess length of time of immersion in the lake, by reference to progression of adipocere, than to address the question of how long the bodies had been floating on the surface. It seems unlikely that they could have been visible and not noticed for some one and a half years, however remote the quarry. It is not known how or if they had been weighted. The boots might have been a factor in maintaining submergence. *Taylor* informs us that in winter an unimpeded body may stay down for up to six weeks. In summer, the period may be as short as two to three days. Children rise more quickly. The answer may be that the bodies in the quarry *were* weighted, or had snagged, or that they had been rising and falling, and by chance had not been spotted when they were uprisen.

The police came knocking at the doors of snug cottages in Winchburgh and Broxburn and asked about two little boys, missing, although not reported, since before Christmas 1911. A suspicion which had lain, repressed, in the depths of their minds, now floated up in the memories of a handful of people who had eschewed gossip and dismissed presentiments of evil. We should not hasten to condemn them.

Patrick Higgins was a red man, coloured by the dust of the brickworks where he worked as a labourer, but not permanently stained like Thomas Hardy's reddleman, whose whole person, horse and cart were saturated with red ochre. His aspect, dark and thick-set as he was, was ogreish as he fried up his meals on a spade and drank rough soup from the pail of his trade. Two small boys called him father, and they had not been seen since one evening in late November, 1911. John was about seven years old at that time and his brother, William, about five. Even their dates of birth had somehow got lost. Patrick, now aged 40, was a man of poor reputation, shiftless, but not of criminal habits. The story was that he had been a fine soldier in India but had been a broken man since the death of his wife – a local woman – in 1910. The reality was that he had already given her a hard time, drinking and neglecting his family. Since her death, his motherless bairns had been the ones to suffer his neglect on their own. They were a burden and a drain on his drinking money.

In January, 1911, John and William were taken into the poorhouse at Dysart. The parish applied to Higgins for their maintenance, and when he refused to comply, he was sent to prison for two months. After his release in August, he boarded them out in Broxburn with a widow, Elizabeth Hynes, whom he had known since he was a boy. He was incorrigible, although earning 24 shillings a week, and never gave the widow a penny. The local Inspector of Poor warned him that he would be taken back to prison unless he mended his ways. By September, they were all three virtually homeless, sometimes reduced to sleeping at the brickyard. These were children at risk, were they not? And the Lord Justice-Clerk was later to berate the parish authorities for failing in their duty towards the paupers for whom they were responsible. Some people took pity on the shabby, cowed little boys, almost unnoticed as they were shuttled from pillar to post by a red, angry man, always in his cups. Then, one evening in November, a kind woman gave them a good, filling meal of Scotch broth.

It was a wet, stormy night in which to be out. Hugh Shields, a miner, saw Higgins and his two sons walking away to the east. Hours afterwards, Paddy came back alone. 'The kids are all right now,' he said over a drink. 'They're on their way to Canada.' James Daly, another miner, also saw Paddy and his boys walking towards Winchburgh, between 7.00 and 8.00pm. Later that night, after about three hours, Paddy Higgins lurched into a bar in Winchburgh, a drowned rat, and out of breath.

He told Daly a different story, a tall one: he and the kids had caught the 8.30 train to Edinburgh, and a lady in the compartment had taken a fancy to one of the boys, and had offered to give him a home. Where one went, the other would have to go, he spoke out straight. Then a second lady who was with her offered to have the other boy. Higgins had hopped off the train at Ratho and run back to Winchburgh in time for a celebratory drink. He had not made a note of the ladies' addresses, but they had his. Paddy had no address, Daly objected, registering somewhere, perhaps, a whiff of suspicion. 'Yes, I have: Patrick Higgins, Winchburgh Brickworks.'

Llewellyn Richards, a third miner, was present and heard

this fairytale. Both he and Daly saw nothing unusual in Paddy's manner. Back he went to his niche at the brickworks to sleep, and there told Alexander Fairnie, a brick-turner, all about the benevolent ladies on the Edinburgh train. Some time afterwards, Fairnie asked him how his boys were getting on. 'They've gone to glory,' Paddy said. Several months after that, he called on Mrs Hynes and told her that they had both drowned. Still no one did anything about it.

It took only a day or two to find Patrick Higgins in 1913. Four policemen, anticipating resistance from the strong red man took him by surprise at a lodging house in Broxburn at 2 o'clock in the morning. The keeper was new, and took them up to a cubicle containing two beds. One of the occupants owned to being the wanted man – 'That's me they want, I believe' – and went quietly, as if he had no cares in the world. He would give no account of himself and said that he did not know where his boys were.

They brought him up at the High Court of Justiciary in Edinburgh on September 11th, 1913, and he comported himself like a soldier on a charge, expressionless and standing to attention when called by name. Coming and going to the dock, he nodded and winked at acquaintances. His plea was Not Guilty: it was argued for him that anyone could have killed the boys. There was no direct evidence. A special defence had been lodged, to the effect that he was insane and not responsible for his actions at the time when he was alleged to have committed the crime.

It appeared that Patrick Higgins suffered, or had suffered, from epilepsy. There was more to his mental profile than drunkenness and problems of personality. It was put, or, more importantly, proved, that epilepsy had been the reason for his discharge from the army. He had, in fact, served six or seven years with the Scottish Rifles in India, so that the affliction could not have been with him as a very young man, and there was some vague talk of injury to the brain.

A general practitioner from Broxburn, Dr Kelso, was brought to say that Higgins' mother had consulted him shortly after Patrick had left the army. She had asked the doctor to see if her son was 'right in the head' because she had woken in the middle of the night to find Patrick standing in the middle of the room, waving a poker in a threatening manner. I suppose that we must take this as true, since the doctor is speaking, and not a mother trying to save her son's life. The mother had witnessed Patrick's 'shaking fits' and seen him fall out of bed, more than once, but his symptoms were complicated by alcohol. A quarryman had several times seen him in the throes of a fit, foaming at the mouth. A former police constable had twice seen him in convulsions in the streets of Winchburgh. An Edinburgh doctor who had examined Higgins while awaiting trial in Calton Jail had found marks of wounds on his head that could well have been incurred during the violent movements of fits. Dr Keay, of Bangour Asylum, could find no evidence of epilepsy and quaintly observed that Higgins was of average intelligence 'for a man of his class'.

It was futile to deny that he was an epileptic, diagnosed and discharged as such from the military service. He apparently took no medication and had not sought the help of Dr Kelso, who would have said if he had been treating him. Drink may have triggered his fits. He himself had instructed his lawyers that he had been free from epilepsy since India, unless he had been drinking. The fact that medical observers saw no sign of epilepsy when they confronted him in his cell in 1913 was neither here nor there. There was, however, no evidence as to frank insanity to support the mother's lurid experience. Doctor after doctor found no symptoms of derangement. All remarked on his cold indifference, but, as the Lord Advocate said 'callousness, cold-bloodedness and deliberate cruelty were not insanity.' Against him, there was the element of premeditation. Why else, except with the intention of harming them, would he have led his children late and in driving rain along a track to nowhere?

The jury returned a unanimous verdict of Guilty, although not until they had asked the judge a series of questions, and they were scrupulous in adding a recommendation to mercy, based on the long gap between the crime and the trial, and also on the lack of expert evidence as to Higgins' mental state at the time of the murders. Patrick Higgins stood to attention as Lord Johnston condemned him to death. He had no chance of a reprieve and on October 1st, 1913, he was hanged and his body buried in a plain black coffin in the prison grounds. The murderer was a lapsed Roman Catholic and Canon Stuart, of St Mary's Cathedral, said prayers beside him to the end. He went very bravely. His last words were – 'The Lord Jesus receive ...' The Canon let it be known that Higgins had confessed to him the justice of his sentence, but if he had been favoured with a full account of his actions at the quarry, he did not say so. 'Drink and, through drink, neglect of religion have brought me down,' he had said, but words of contrition relating to his lost boys are somehow missing.

After the hangman, John Ellis, had done his job and the black flag had been hoisted, in the world outside, the crowds who had stood on the top of Calton Hill were moving off for a day at Musselburgh Races. Others scrambled down from the monumental canons. It was said that a blind fiddler played 'The Lost Chord'.

Sir Sidney Smith recorded a piece of doggerel that appeared in a university magazine:

> Two bodies found in a lonely mere,
> Converted into adipocere.
> Harvey, when called in to see 'em,
> Said, 'Just what I need for my museum'.

Times and manners change, but the final episode of the Hopetoun Quarry tragedy would now be regarded as unacceptable practice by professional men. In 1913, a spot of latter-day 'body-snatching' was a jolly jape, all, of course, in the best interests of science. During the autopsy in the Linlithgow mortuary, Dr Smith was taken with the idea of keeping specimens of the perfect adipocere formation for teaching purposes. Professor Harvey Littlejohn, approving the idea, actually co-operated by asking the two police officers present to go outside with him. Surreptitiously, Smith then packed up the two heads, a leg and an arm from each, and all the internal organs, and the two doctors travelled back to Edinburgh by train with the parcels on the luggage-rack, an embarrassing and dubious procedure in itself. The specimens were displayed in the Forensic Medicine Museum at the University. No parent was left alive to grieve and make protest.

As a timely reminder that the dissection of human corpses has not always proceeded smoothly since the days of Burke and Hare, we might care to contemplate the bad riot of 1831, when a crowd demolished the Anatomical School in Aberdeen, a building recently erected by Dr Andrew Moir in St Andrew's Street, at the back of Gordon's Hospital. The people called the brave new edifice the 'Anatomical Theatre' and they feared what went on inside its walls.

A dog it was that lit the tinder when it scented something interesting in the loose soil at the back of the school and began to dig. Some boys playing nearby raised the alarm and soon there was a sizeable crowd as recognisable fragments of a human body were excavated. There was a howl of execration and several medical students were seen making a hasty exit. Dr Moir stayed inside until the door was forced. He escaped, but was followed to his lodgings and even there had to jump out of a back window.

Meanwhile, at the Anatomical School, three dead bodies were revealed, stretched, stripped and striated on boards. All the equipment of the place was now destroyed or carried away. Officers were called and they directed the bodies to be taken out. When the mangled remnants were brought into the open air and laid on the ground, there were yells and cries for vengeance. A few rags of clothing were pulled on to the bodies and they were removed.

'Burn the house!' they cried. 'Down with the Burking shop!' A fierce fire was kindled within, stoked by shavings, fir, and tar barrel staves. Outside, a crowd was undermining the back wall of the building with two large planks, one used as a battering-ram, the other as a lever. The entire wall collapsed with a tremendous crash. The front wall came under attack. The heat from the blaze was intense. The Provost and magistrates came to the inferno, with a brigade of special constables, and a party of the 79th Regiment was marched out of barracks and held in reserve in Gordon's Hospital. There were cheers as the gables collapsed, along with the roof. Thousands of people were said to be present, not all riff-raff, by any means, which indicates the strength of public opinion. Three rioters were put to their trial, during which the Advocate-Depute allowed that carelessness by the medical gentlemen had led to the disturbance.

CHAPTER 16
THE POISONOUS PUDDOCKS

The unexpected visitor with a smile on his face and a packet of arsenic in his pocket was stoutly-named George Thom, a guest who stayed to dinner and left as soon as he possibly could. His hosts, a family of four, symmetrically divided into two brothers and two sisters, were living in peace and harmony in deep countryside at Burnside, in Keig, Aberdeenshire. Although a rare caller, George was no stranger, being related by marriage. Once the Mitchells had been six, but two members had broken away from the constellation: Jean had gone to marry George Thom, and one brother had died, leaving a considerable legacy, which was apportioned among the five survivors.

There had been a former Mrs Thom, but she had died years previously, leaving issue. George had married Jean a decent time after she had come into her share of the inheritance, and borne her away to his farm at Harthill, Newmills. All rejoiced. If, at the age of 61, he were a little long in the tooth, and perhaps Jeanie was too, he was well respected, a good man who had worked his farm for donkey's years.

However, something went wrong in his mind in 1821, when he began to ruminate about the four parts of the legacy which were held by the unmarried Mitchells. From the seed of the envy, the need grew to an acorn like a diseased pineal gland lodged deep in the brain, and then it swelled and branched and took over all parts of his mind until he was eaten away by a plan of outrageous simplicity. In one act of mass murder he would eliminate the entire Mitchell clan for ever and Jeanie would inherit the fruit of his cleverness. Poison would be the means, and after some initial difficulty he acquired a stock of arsenic sufficient to kill a bullock or two.

Thus equipped, he turned up at Burnside, on his own, one Saturday evening in August, and made himself amiable, although he had not visited since his marriage. The Mitchells were surprised, but pleased, and made him welcome. He gave no reason for his arrival: one would have expected some kind of excuse, but he was too preoccupied with sending them all to kingdom come. Their hospitality and attentions were a nuisance to him. It was arranged that he was to stay the night, after supper, as he had frequently done in the past (presumably when he was courting Jean) always sharing William's bed. This time, he was very anxious to sleep in the kitchen, but William insisted on the old arrangement, which was not the way that Thom had planned it. He said that he would have to get up early, and would not, absolutely not, be persuaded to stay to breakfast, because he was expected for that meal at the farm, Mains of Cluny, on his way home.

James Mitchell, whose bed was in the recess in the kitchen, woke in the early hours when he heard footsteps near the press, but could not see who it was, because his bed-shutters were closed. The furtive figure was, of course, George Thom in the execution of his blunt device to wipe out the Mitchells, tipping the contents of his little packet into the saltcellar and stirring frantically.

Helen Mitchell found him alone in the kitchen later, about to take his departure, and he was shaking some crumbs of bread and cheese on the table with something white about them. She asked him what it was, but, not being gifted at improvisation, he made no reply. William gave him a piece of loaf-bread (wheaten loaf) which he wrapped up in his napkin, but did not put in his pocket. The import here is that the arsenic had leaked from its wrapping in his pocket and contaminated remnants of old ploughman's lunches. As usual, he was looking after Number One. Perhaps the crumbs were swept up and thrown on the fire, since there were no reports of ailing wee beasties.

Then George Thom left Burnside and ate a hearty breakfast at the Cluny farm. On his way back to Harthill, mightily refreshed, he met an acquaintance and told him that he had been very unwell and must have eaten something that morning, or at supper the night before, which had upset him. If he had not used a crow's feather to make himself vomit, he said, he would have surely died. This was a palpable falsehood which seemed like a good idea at the time, but was to return to haunt him. He was much more successful as a solid man of few words.

Their guest gone, Mary Mitchell, the other sister, made pottage (porridge) prepared with milk, not water, and the obligatory pinch of salt. The whole family had some. William, Helen and Mary noticed nothing unusual. William ate a lot; it was Sacrament Sunday and dinner would be rather late. James, however, was obviously sensitive to arsenic. He had intended to tuck in, but he did not enjoy the pottage that morning, objecting to its 'sweetish, sickening taste'. Most people can detect no taste, as has been noted repeatedly in criminal cases. If noticed at all, it is likely to be sensed as acrid or bitter, although that old authority, Professor Christison, did say that it was insipid or sweetish.

James was already feeling sick. He dressed and felt worse, but forced himself to walk to church. On the way, he felt so ill that he wondered about going home. When he was in his pew, a strange blackness suddenly clouded around his field of vision and he seemed to be going blind. After he had sat at the Lord's Table, he swayed out into the graveyard, where he came upon his brother, William, who said that he was very sick. William went back into church, but James crawled home, vomiting all the way. When he reached the house, with all his insides burning, he found that both his sisters had been sick, too. William came in with the worse symptoms, complaining of great pain, with a swelling in his chest, reaching up to his throat.

Somehow, they all survived the night. Next day, Helen had numb feet, a burning pain by her heart, great thirst, and anguish in her left eyelid. Mary had lost all sensation in her legs, from the knees downward. On the Tuesday, James lost the use of one arm and both feet. These three afflicted gradually recovered, but not William, who lingered for one week, until the following Lord's Day. By then, he had lost all use of his arms and was nearly blind, his eyes blood-red. James, who shared his bed in that simple household, tearfully described his last moments: 'He rose to look for a drink, returned to his bed and lay down, stretched himself, and gave a terrible groan, then lay quiet. He was in a cold, deep sweat.' James went to his sisters and told them that William was 'gaen to wear awa' out amo' them'.

The Mitchells did, as it turned out, suspect that George had poisoned them, but they wanted to keep the scandal secret. They were quiet people and they did not want a fuss. Jeanie was married to the man. The day before William's funeral, George and Jean arrived at Burnside without being asked, and were ill-received. James told them to go, as they had already done enough mischief in the house. Apparently, some neighbours, acutely suspicious, had said that they would not attend the funeral if Thom and Jean were allowed to stay.

As they were about to leave, unwillingly, Helen invited Jean to view the corpse. She did so, gladly, but George Thom refused, in the grip, no doubt, of the host of superstitions attendant on the encounter between dead victim and hypocritical murderer, and Jean chose that moment to tell him, 'Nelly [Helen] says my brother was poisoned.' That were possible, said George Thom, as poison might have got in the burn from the toads or the puddocks (frogs). Not so, was Helen's trump-card: the pottage was made with milk, not water from the burn. Thom's preposition was less fantastic than it now appears. Frogs are not poisonous, but there is some poison in toads, and in 1821 many beliefs from folk-lore still made the harmless creature an object of fear and rendered it liable to persecution, like the witch with which it was identified. In medieval times, bandits sometimes forced a toad into the mouth of a hapless traveller.

Let Frank Buckland, the great Victorian naturalist, describe the poison of toads: 'Like the lizards, they have glands in their skin, which secrete a white highly-acid fluid, and just behind the head are seen two eminences like split beans: if these be pressed, this acid fluid will come out – only let the operator mind that it does not get into his eyes, for it generally comes out with a jet. There are also other glands dispersed throughout the skin. A dog will never take a toad in his mouth, and the reason is that this glandular secretion burns his tongue and lips...'

Anyway, was Thom's parting-shot, he, too, had been taken very ill and had lain three days in bed, all swollen. Such a terrible crime was bound to come out, however, and on the night of August 31st, George and Jean Thom were both apprehended as they slept. Jean was discharged after she had made an exculpatory statement. In September, Thom was tried at the Circuit Court. Mr Barton, druggist in Aberdeen, notably stated that on about August 17th, a man who resembled the prisoner in the dock came to his shop to buy arsenic for rats, but as he did not know him, he actually refused to serve him – a refreshing change from all those other gung-ho suppliers of the past. The actual source of the poison was not traced. We may safely assume that Thom tipped the whole lot – perhaps one ounce – into the salt. It was not recorded that the salt was analysed, and the reason for that is that everyone, including the jury, believed that Thom had doctored the pottage, not the salt. It was not until he confessed, after the verdict of Guilty by a majority, that it became known that the salt had been the true medium. After sentence of death had been passed upon him, he carelessly brushed his hat with a steady hand and remarked to members of the bar, 'Gentlemen, I am as innocent as any of you sitting here.'

Once he learnt that there was to be no reprieve, his attitude changed, and he signed a document which entirely exonerated his wife. Gossip flowed around the district: a man named Thomas Gill had been found dead in the harbour at Aberdeen, in November, 1817, and an attempt was now made to link him to the murder. He denied it, and claimed that he had been ill in bed at the time. When his last Sunday on earth came round, they let his sons and a daughter visit him. As one of his sons was embracing him in an agony of grief, he slipped a note into his hand, begging him to sneak in some poison so that he could die before the hangman came. The son went home, shocked by the idea of suicide, and wrote him a letter of refusal. The authorities were told, and from then on the condemned man was always attended by two warders.

He was too weak to stand at the scaffold, a quavering, quivering figure in his shroud, before they hanged him on November 16th, 1821. A part of the 103rd Psalm was sung – 'The Lord is merciful and gracious, slow to anger, and plenteous in mercy ...' The Aberdeenshire Militia escorted his body to the college for dissection by Drs Skene and Ewing. The corpse was subjected to a series of galvanic experiments which were written up in a scientific journal. Better the wry-necked body of a hanged man than a live animal. By 1821, research was moving on to the nervous system, but, by a curious irony, Luigi Galvani (1737-98) whose whole research was directed towards ascertaining the relation of animal muscle to electricity, had been experimenting on frogs.

CHAPTER 17
THE TRAM RIDE

The 11.45 tram from Buckhaven to East Wemyss swayed and rattled along the road near the coast. Two passengers on that cold, February morning were drawn together by fate, or fell design. The speculation matters, because the robbery and murder that were to come to pass, quite soon now, were either most cunningly premeditated, or were the acts of wild opportunism and impulse. The killer did not deny what he did, but would say only that, 'I did not know what I was doing. My head was a blank.'

Was Alexander Edmonstone a stranger to his victim, Michael Brown, or, both living in the Fifeshire village of East Wemyss, were they acquainted? Evidence does not seem to have been led that they knew each other. Their backgrounds were different and there was a significant age gap. Michael Swinton Brown, 15 rising 16, was a very nice-looking boy with a future, the much prized son of a stonemason, improving himself as a fledgling in the world of commerce. He worked as an apprentice clerk for Messrs G & J Johnston, linen manufacturers, whose dark, satanic mills lay along the seashore at East Wemyss.

The firm banked inconveniently at the branch of the Royal Bank of Scotland which was situated a mile or so away at the neighbouring fishing village of Buckhaven. It was Michael Brown's important duty every Friday to take the tram to the bank and return with the firm's wages in cash, amounting this morning to £85, carried in a brown leather bag which, no doubt, proclaimed exactly what it was – a money bag. Alone, the unprotected pseudo-adult made the regular journey, with no variation. It must have been common knowledge, but East Wemyss was a quiet, respectable, tight-knit mining community, unacquainted with the worst type of crime.

Alexander Edmonstone's family were incomers, having moved from Edinburgh to their home at the east end of the village in 1902. He was a young man of 23, a miner or carter, with a tendency to be unemployed. His real interest was motor cars, and he also liked nice clothes, but his problem in life was that he was chronically pecuniarily embarrassed. He had no criminal form whatsoever. Of late, he had not been feeling particularly well. The headaches were killing him.

The date of doom was Friday, February 19th, 1909. Edmonstone behaved unusually that morning. Rising early, he seemed excited, and announced that he was going to try to get a job on the steamers plying between Methil and Hamburg, and might not be back. He took with him a few belongings, which would seem to indicate that he had a bag of some kind with him, but none was ever mentioned, and left home at 10.30am. Methil Dock was about one mile up the coast from Buckhaven and theoretically he could have gone there first by tram and been quickly turned away by the shipping company, but by 11.30am he was undoubtedly in Buckhaven, standing at the corner opposite the Royal Bank of Scotland. Henry Kildair, a Buckhaven miner, knew Edmonstone, and, spotting him there, had a brief conversation with him. The theory was that he was loitering in order to catch Michael Brown as he left the bank, but since Buckhaven was a small place, he could have been doing what unemployed young men do naturally in the town centre.

Brown's day, so far, had been uneventful. He had left his home in Parkhill Terrace, Station Road – where the trams ran past his door – and walked down School Wynd to the factory. Later, he caught the tram and was in Buckhaven at about

11.20am, leaving the bank with his heavy bag at 11.30am ...
On the corner, Edmonstone suddenly stopped talking to
Kildair, saying that he was going to catch the tram home.
James Goldie recognized Brown and Edmonstone, *walking
along the tramlines together* towards Muiredge stopping
place. Peter Adamson saw Brown board the tramcar at
11.45am, 'looking solemn' and holding a brown leather bag
tightly, followed by Edmonstone.

Alex Chalmers, the tram conductor, said that a boy sat
next to a man in his early 20s. This is an ambiguous statement.
Was there an element of choice? Who joined whom? Brown
was a polite boy. The tram might not have been crowded,
because when the aforesaid Adamson alighted at the Rosie pit
in East Wemyss, only three passengers were left – Brown,
Edmonstone, and a young girl. Sitting together, the
presumption is that words were exchanged, and the subject of
the brown leather bag might have been raised by either party.

The conductor said that the boy and the man got off the
tram at Station Road at the top of School Wynd at exactly
11.54am. The boy left first, the man following close behind.
Was Brown trying to shake him off? Was he becoming a
nuisance, his conversation an embarrassment in some way? Or
was Brown feeling suspicious, frightened, even? If he had been
really apprehensive, he could have gone straight to his home
in Station Road, instead of heading for the factory.
Edmonstone was going in the right direction for *his* home,
which would have been reassuring. Several others saw the pair
going fast down the Wynd, one behind the other, Brown
always in front. George Black actually exchanged greetings in
the vernacular with Edmonstone. As they proceeded, it was
afterwards postulated that the older man was hanging back in
order not to be seen with the boy. It was a busy time of day and
School Wynd was well used. The pair do not seem to have been
talking to each other. The last sighting was by Mrs Alice
Warrender, who watched them briefly from her kitchen

window at her house in School Wynd at 12 o'clock. She knew Michael.

At the end of the Wynd, there was a men's public lavatory, totally roofless, entered through a narrow, two feet seven inch open gap in the continuous wall of the lane. Inside, there was a small yard with the urinal to the right, running parallel to the outside wall, and one doored cubicle, also open to the sky, to the back, on the left. It was most definitely not in a hidden or even secluded place, with East Wemyss school very close, on the opposite side of the thoroughfare. Mrs Warrender was unlucky enough to have a view of the public convenience from her window. She stopped watching Brown and Edmonstone when they were feet away from the ugly little building, but she had noticed that the boy was on the inside of the Wynd, nearest to the urinal.

Those were unsuspicious days and there was no whisper of homosexuality attached to the proceedings at that time, as far as is known. This was scarcely an opportunity for an assignation, since Brown was due back at the factory with the wages at midday and was expected home for dinner at 12.30pm. He was always a good boy. Edmonstone could have calculated that the latrine was the last available place for him to make his strike, although he was taking the risk of being discovered in felonious act, *or* the gap in the wall suddenly presented itself as an unplanned expedient.

There were no witnesses to what happened next. Most likely, Edmonstone pushed the boy through the entrance; or Brown wanted to use the lavatory and Edmonstone followed him in; or Brown went in of his own volition in the hope that Edmonstone would walk on and leave him alone; or both agreed to use the lavatory in a friendly, masculine manner. Once inside, the man attacked the boy fiercely, and he resisted, but had no chance. Edmonstone knew that he had been seen repeatedly with Brown that morning, and he battered him to death. It is most unsatisfactory that the weapon was never identified. It was thought that the boy's head had been banged on the walls and the floors. Two separate methods of killing were undertaken: a grubby white handkerchief was tightly knotted around Brown's neck and his cap was crammed into his mouth. It was difficult to stifle that young life.

There was blood everywhere. A large pool lay just inside the entrance. Edmonstone *was* nearly caught; once he dragged his victim into the cubicle, and the second time, a man actually heard gurglings coming from the cubicle, but thought that it was the schoolboys, up to tricks.

Alexander Edmonstone fled from the scene, with his booty. There was no point in going home. Following the course of a stream, Back Burn, (according to the map, as also in 'Back Dykes', but generally given more atmospherically as Black Burn) he escaped to the outskirts of the village, where he emptied the contents of the money bag into his pockets and hid it in some rocks between Court Cave and McDuff's Castle.

Meanwhile, after 15 minutes or thereabouts, a young lad was the first to set eyes on what remained of Michael Brown. Identification was not immediate. His employers did not realize that their clerk was missing until 1.30pm. William Johnston only recognized the body after being shown a pencil and the tram ticket, which was still in the hand. The news of the murder devastated the entire district. Work stopped and School Wynd was jammed with local people. If Spring-Heeled Jack had leapt into that wide-open building the panic could not have been more intense.

Edmonstone was under suspicion, and he had vanished. A Wanted poster was distributed and it was seen that his appearance was almost comically distinctive. His hair was auburn, three teeth were missing from the front of his upper jaw, and AE was tattooed on his right forearm. Bloodhounds were brought to the scene, in a wry memory of Burgho and Barnaby, thwarted trackers of Jack the Ripper, but with no success, since the scent was cold. All the ships in dock locally were searched, but Edmonstone had had other plans. Fleeing towards Strathmiglo, he had borrowed a brush from a woman pulling hay from a stack, and coolly removed, as far as he could, dark stains from the knees of his trousers. After walking 12 miles north-west of East Wemyss, he entered the drapery at the village and bought a fine new stylish outfit. They were so pleased with the order that they threw in a free tie.

Then on to Strathmiglo Station, splendidly attired, where he caught a train to Perth and spent the night at a Temperance Hotel. He required the maid to clean his very dirty boots. The next morning, after a sustaining breakfast of ham and eggs, he took a train to Glasgow. The police were getting closer all the time. He could not stay. Taking lodgings at 113 Renfield Street, he promptly went out, leaving two parcels on the bed. He had paid for his room. Moving on to Paisley, he planted a faked suicide note on the parapet of the bridge over the River Cart. Just like a false Jack the Ripper confessor, he wrote in red ink: *I murdered Mickey Brown – AE. You will find my body at the foot of water near by. I filled my pockets with stones. I bid goodbye to mother. Goodbye – Alexander Edmonstone.*

The landlady in Glasgow became suspicious and opened the parcels. They contained bloodstained clothing. The River Cart was carefully dragged. A second Wanted poster was issued, offering a reward of £100. One month passed since the crime, and Edmonstone had, in fact, escaped to England, but the posters followed him, and he looked much the same. He was now calling himself Albert Edwards, to chime with his tattoo, and living in a boarding-house at 12 Brunswick Street, Chorlton-cum-Hardy, a suburb of Manchester. He could not disguise his Scottish accent, and he lived on lies. It was noticed that he had difficulty in sleeping and eating. He bought rounds for everyone as if he had money to burn, and kept his valuables in a locked Gladstone bag.

A new lodger, a young hawker named John Atherton, came to live at the boarding-house. On March 21st, while at Whitworth police station in connection with his application for a hawker's licence, he happened to be studying the £100 reward poster, and thought that he recognized the photographs. He had a drink with 'Albert Edwards' and casually asked him for the right time, whereupon Edmonstone produced a silver watch. Just such a watch had been described on the poster as having been stolen from Michael Brown. On March 22nd, the police went in force to Brunswick Street. When he was challenged – 'What do you know of the murder of a young boy in Fifeshire, Scotland?' – Edmonstone closed his eyes and blocked out the moment that he had been dreading. 'It's all right,' he said and raised his hands in submission. As they led him away, he told his landlady, Mrs Bridgewood, 'Don't worry about me, Ma, I'll be all right.'

But of course he was not going to be all right. Goodness knows what he imagined was going to help him, but his plea of insanity was never going to be effective. That plea was still frowned on in the Scottish and English courts and Lord Guthrie was not the judge to protect him. It was put for him that the substantial illness of epilepsy lay behind the headaches, and that his grandfather had died a lunatic in Morningside Asylum. He himself had been treated in hospital for 'sunstroke', and, as it happens, we now know that so-called sunstroke could be schizophrenia – as in the case of the famous insane artist, Richard Dadd. But Edmonstone was not mad enough for mercy and he was executed at Perth on July 6th, 1909.

CHAPTER 18
THE TOOTH-FIEND

Biggar, in Lanarkshire, was a nice quiet little town in 1967. Nimbyism must have afflicted some of the inhabitants in 1962, when Loaningdale Approved School was planted in their midst. It was hard on parents of teenage girls in the locality, because warning them to stay away from slick youths, often from the city, and emboldened by their peers, was bound to be counter-productive. The Gordon Hay case well illustrates the difficulty of predicting which young male will turn out to be a serious sexual murderer. A 17-year-old, he had been sent to Loaningdale for the offence of breaking into a factory, but his propensity for extreme violence had not become overt, although other boys were somewhat afraid of him.

There was a progressive element abroad in the school, a hint of a therapeutic community, with all, staff and inmates, committed to the common good and the improvement of the individual. Discipline had to be in place but it was not oppressive: doors were not kept locked and inmates were allowed out in the town during daylight hours. The Deputy Headmaster, Clifford Lloyd Davis, admitted that boys occasionally sneaked out to meet girls without permission. Interesting details of the rules and routines were to emerge. After the worst had happened, there was a curtailment of humane freedoms, as there had to be when mutual trust had broken down.

On the evening of Saturday, August 5th, 1967, a group of boys had been allowed out to the cinema and then to a visiting fair, supervised by a master. Gordon Hay was there, bored and ripe for mischief, until he saw Linda Peacock approaching with a friend. He had already spoken to Linda three weeks previously, and was interested in her. The other girl, obeying the usual parental warning, walked on, but Linda had a few words with Hay. This was, it was thought, the opportunity for a secret tryst to be arranged for the following evening. As he slipped proudly back to his friends, Hay informed them – and this is a euphemism – that he would like to have sexual congress with the girl. It was men's talk.

Linda Peacock was still at school, aged 15, horse-mad, at an era when showjumping was all the rage and repeatedly shown on television. She was a competent rider, winning rosettes at local shows, and could well have gone on to a career in horses. An only child, she lived with her parents, who apparently were not at all young, in a picturesque cottage at Carwood, about one and a half miles from Biggar. She had a boyfriend, although that does not necessarily have its present meaning. As was to become known to the whole country, sexual congress was not a part of her short experience of life. It was said that she had been out with another youth from the school, but no harm had been done.

Sunday at Loaningdale, far from home, if that mattered, and without the milestones of lessons, must have dragged and made worse the pubescent frustrations of the 30 or so pent up youths. There was some relaxation of the rules. In the evening, there were games, and the boys could watch television until 9.00pm, when they had to go to their dormitories, clean their boots, wash, and put on their pyjamas and dressing-gowns, which they wore to supper at 9.15pm. Then they could go back to their dormitories or sit around until 10.00pm, which was bedtime. A housemaster patrolled the dormitories from about 10.30 to 10.45, to check that all the boys were safely in bed, and turn off the lights.

Gordon Hay had other ideas. On Sunday, August 6th, he

had played football and then, according to his own account, after the whist drive, in the evening, he had changed from his day clothes into pyjama trousers, a white casual shirt, and boots. He had supper at about 9.30pm before watching *The Untouchables* in the television room. That programme, one would have thought, with its emphasis on power and violence, could have been a potent trigger for emotional eruption in an unstable individual. Just before 10.00pm, he happened to be in the dining-room, watching three boys playing cards, and talking to them until 10.25. He was in bed by 10.30. However, according to an unnamed 15-year-old boy, one of Hay's dormitory mates, Hay was missing from the school between about 9.55 and 10.45pm. Hay's dressing-gown was seen lying on his bed, with his pyjamas in his locker at 10.15.

What is horrible about his movements is what he carried with him. It was thought that he took his dressing-gown cord to the meeting with Linda Peacock, and strong circumstantial evidence indicated that he arrived at the rendezvous equipped with a ghastly weapon – a boat-hook brought back from summer camp by the 15-year-old, which had fascinated Hay. He could have intended merely to show it to Linda, to impress her, or he could have planned to threaten her with it, to get his way. Or he could have carried it like a totem, to feel empowered. He could have been totally sexually inexperienced.

He moved fast, to be at the gates of St Mary's Cemetery by about 10.00pm. Linda Peacock was still, riskily, in town. She had spent the day at stables, and had left home at 8.00pm, when a young male lodger had given her a lift into the centre of Biggar. He offered to pick her up later and drive her home, but this was not what she wanted, and she refused, saying rather tartly that he need not bother as he had let her down previously that week over such an arrangement. He watched as she left him, joined another girl, and walked up the main street with her. He never saw her again, but an elderly man, who knew Linda, had a long conversation with her about horses at the door of his house in Carwood Road. They talked for 20 minutes, and he had the impression that she was killing time. She had left her girl companion at 9.30.

Linda Peacock was last seen alive walking alone along Carwood Road, where the cemetery wall skirted the road. The gate lay ahead, and, if she continued, Loaningdale School gate. Home, if that were her objective, was a lonely mile ahead. At times between 10.02 and 10.08pm, witnesses saw 'a couple' in the area. One driver noticed in the half-light a young man facing towards Biggar and a young woman who looked if she had been, or was, walking away from Biggar. A female passenger in another passing car thought that she saw a young man with his back to her and his left shoulder forward as though he were leaning against a tombstone. 'Well,' she said to her husband and son, 'I've seen many a thing, but never a couple courting in a graveyard!' Screams were heard from the direction of the cemetery at 10.20pm.

Meanwhile, back at Loaningdale, the two other occupants of Hay's dormitory, after realizing that he was missing at 9.55 actually searched the school for him, without telling a master or being seen by one. The reason for their concern is not entirely clear but the fact that the fisherman's hook was no longer in the wardrobe, where it should have been, could have contributed to their feeling that something untoward was up. They scrambled into their beds at 10.30, expecting the housemaster to appear at any moment. One boy went to sleep immediately. The other – the 15-year-old – was still awake when Gordon Hay burst in 10 to 15 minutes later, wearing his outdoor clothing. He seemed excited, his hair was dishevelled, his face dirty, and the knees of his jeans looked as if he had been working in the garden and had been kneeling down. He washed as fast as he could and jumped into bed just in time before lights out.

Linda's parents, waiting in their cottage, were getting

worried. At 11.00pm, the lodger came home and was surprised to hear that she was not safely back. He drove straight out again and called at various relatives' houses in Biggar. They searched the quiet, dark, lamp-lit streets, but it was no good, and soon the police had to be told that Linda Peacock was missing.

The next day, early, at 6.40am, two constables discovered her body in St Mary's Cemetery, lying beside a gravestone and almost concealed by an overhanging yew tree. Shreds of foliage had fluttered down on to the stricken girl. Two open wounds of different length had been inflicted on the crown of her head and she had been strangled afterwards by a ligature, which was not still present. There was a mark of another ligature, also absent, on the left wrist, and a burn made after death indicated that it had been burnt off, not cut. It looked as if a petrol-fuelled cigarette lighter had been used and caused a coating of black carbon over the burn. Gordon Hay had a lighter of that type, and no knife. Perhaps penknives were forbidden.

The clothing on the upper part of the body only had been pulled about, and there was a severe bite-mark on the right breast. The girl had strong nails and a short fibre from sisal string, bloody, was lodged in the left forefinger nail. A piece of sisal string, knotted at both ends, and a slipknot, were found hanging in the yew tree. Two three-inch-round bloodstains situated 10 yards away suggested that Linda had received the two blows to the head but had even so, been able to run, being fit and athletic, before being strangled. Coins, a comb and a purse plotted her flight.

Chief Superintendent Muncie directed an investigation which revealed the multiplicity of activity associated with such an apparently peaceful little town. The fact that it was high summer did not help. By sheer bad luck, the travelling fair had moved on, and all the showmen had to be located. As if that were not enough, there was a popular caravan site, packed with regular, weekend, and casual visitors. Many youths from surrounding villages had been drawn into Biggar. Four young men had come from Edinburgh by car and had roared round the streets and accosted several girls. An itinerant knife-grinder had to be carefully eliminated, since he was known actually to have called at the Peacocks' cottage on the Sunday afternoon, spoken to Linda in person, and asked for a place to sleep. He had been directed to a nearby derelict house. He had in his possession quantities of sisal string, but he was not the one. A certain farm labourer who had a local reputation for interfering with girls had been seen walking along Carwood Road on Sunday evening, and he had to be rigorously questioned. The Peacocks' lodger was in an uncomfortable position, but he was soon beyond suspicion, as was Linda's boyfriend, who lived in a nearby town. Promising, but quickly discarded, was one of the travelling showmen: a constable recognized his name as that of a man who had attacked a young girl in a park near the cemetery, with intent to ravish.

The proximity of Loaningdale Approved School to the scene of crime was not lost on Superintendent Muncie. It was established that a running boy could get from the yew tree to the rear door of the school in one minute and 43 seconds. A large team of five detective officers headed by a detective inspector was sent in. They were not pleased to learn that some of Sunday's clothing had already been put in the wash, and that included the boys' jeans. Every boy was accounted for at the relevant time by his dormitory mates and teachers. The police also worked on a roster of all inmates since the opening of the school five years previously, since, pleasantly to relate, many of them came back to Biggar. Other police forces painstakingly checked their movements.

The enquiry narrowed by Wednesday 9th, when the team concentrating on the school 'broke' the 15-year-old boy, who now admitted that he had lied about Gordon Hay. There was a strong culture of not 'grassing' at Loaningdale, and he and the other boy had been afraid of Hay, but felt able to talk because he had just been transferred to a new school, 250 miles away, that Wednesday morning. The reason for the transfer was not disclosed, but it must have been looked into by the police. Both the boys said that Hay had approached them on the Monday, when the detectives arrived, and told them to say that they were all in bed at 10.00pm.

The dormitory was searched, and the boat-hook was found in the wardrobe, innocent of blood. Medical opinion was that it could have caused the wounds to the head. The sisal string could have pointed to Hay. On the Saturday, one of the two other boys had taught him a game with a piece of such string, called the 'see-saw trick'. Apparently it required two people: a loop was passed round the wrists of one, and, after a few intermediate movements, it was taken in the teeth of both, and a strange see-saw effect was obtained. Hay had been obsessed with the game, like a child, and had kept the string in his pocket.

Police officers were sent to interview Gordon Hay and bring him back to Lanarkshire. He was remarkably cool and detached. 'I was never out of the school,' he kept saying. There was no sign of an inclination to confess, although when, eventually, it was put to him that he should speak out if he had some illicit purpose for sneaking out of the school, not connected with the murder, and he was asked if he wished to change his statement, Muncie saw him wipe a tear from his eye as he said again, 'I canna mind of being out of the school that night, sir.'

The police found a two to three inch piece of charred dressing-gown cord in an old, broken-down, brick-built incinerator in the school grounds. The proposition was that this was the material used to strangle Linda Peacock, and again the disturbing question arises as to why Gordon Hay would have taken it with him to meet the girl. It surely cannot have been possible to identify it as belonging to him in particular. It must have been easy to confirm that waste of this kind was not routinely burnt in the incinerator, although it must be said that objects do migrate around in institutions.

Asked about his dressing-gown, Hay claimed that he had not been wearing one at all on Sunday night, because they had not given him one on his return from leave on the Saturday. As a matter of fact, he said, he never wore a cord, and his had lain in a drawer in his dormitory until a fortnight before the murder, when he had thrown it into a wastepaper basket.

A small spot of blood was found on one of his boots, and another on the leg of one pair of his trousers, but this was 1967, and nothing could be done with the traces, which were insufficient for the grouping techniques then available. The winder was missing from his wristwatch, and the glass was scratched. He claimed that he had damaged the watch recently while polishing a dormitory floor at his new school. The police went off to inspect the dormitory and were told that it had not been in use, and had been kept locked, since Hay had worked there, using only soft dusters. If Hay were telling the truth, the winder should have been, or could have been, on the floor, but it was not found. Then the cemetery was searched for the winder, but even four specially 'souped-up' vacuum cleaners contributed by a Hoover factory failed to syphon it out of the grass. Ten men vacuumed for hours and the contents were sifted on tables under imported lighting.

The bite-mark left by the murderer was becoming the bright hope of the investigation, and, indeed, the scientific component of the case was to go on to establish absolutely the acceptance by the courts of the little-known discipline of forensic odontology. Photographs had been taken at the scene of crime and it was now a matter of comparing Gordon Hay's dental characteristics. He agreed to have his dental impressions taken. A further 28 boys who had been resident at the school over the relevant weekend agreed to the same procedure, which was carried out at the Glasgow Dental Hospital by staff working through their lunch-hour. The intention was to prevent Dr Warren Harvey, an expert in the rare science, and Professor Keith Simpson, of Guy's Hospital, who had been called in, from knowing the identity of the main suspect. Five boys were recalled for further impressions, but the results were unsatisfactory.

The original photographs had shown five bruises or bite-marks, and the largest mark, a dark oval, had been looking the most promising. It seems curious to the layman that two of the five marks looked exceptional, being small, dark rings with pale centres, but that their importance was only now appreciated. The experts had not found a description of such pale-centred marks in the relevant literature, but, then, what was available for reference was mostly in foreign works, particularly Swedish or Japanese.

Now, on re-examination of the whole range of casts taken, it was seen that the model which turned out to be that provided by Gordon Hay explained the phenomenon. The tip of the upper and lower right canines contained a distinctive small but definite pit. Canine teeth are not supposed to have pits. A third impression was taken of Hay's teeth, after a sheriff's warrant had been obtained, and the pits were minutely photographed. All oblivious of the significance of his dental abnormality, he was, in fact, extremely co-operative and also positively enjoyed having his prized tattoo mark photographed.

The public analyst was consulted on the fluorine content of the water which Hay had drunk as a boy. Dr Harvey established that the little craters were caused by hypocalcination, i.e. this was a developmental fault, not caused by caries or wear. With the remarkable attention to detail which characterized the case, Harvey examined 1,000 canines in 342 boys aged 16 to 17, and isolated only two with pits, and none with pits in the same mouth.

Gordon Hay was arrested on a warrant for murder. A special defence of alibi was lodged: other boys were to swear that he was inside the school premises between 9.00pm and midnight on Sunday, August 6th. The trial began at the High Court in Edinburgh on February 26th, 1968. It was a fierce fight with the bite-mark at the core of the case. The Crown cited 105 witnesses. The defence, naturally, picked away at the newness of forensic odontology, but, as the judge commented in his summing up, 'There must, of course, always be a first time for everything.'

There was a weak area in the Crown case: Gösta Gustavson, who had written what was then the only full textbook on the discipline, had suggested that a minimum of four or five adjacent teeth corresponding with bite-marks were desirable for a positive identification, and here there were only three, and they were not adjacent. The defence made full use of this point, but the rare canine pits were to win the day. The Solicitor-General said that there would be few if any people with a similar dental structure to Hay's in Britain, or indeed anywhere in the world. Dr Harvey used a ballpoint pen with the ball retracted to demonstrate on the fine skin below his thumbnail how, on pressure, a mark was produced that was pale in the centre.

Gordon Hay spoke up boldly in the witness box, and denied everything. He still denied having been out of the school on the Sunday, although he did admit to illicit absences on other occasions to meet girls in Biggar. It was another Loaningdale boy who had talked to Linda at the fairground, and he did not even know who she was. It was another boy who had fancied the boat-hook as a good weapon, and he himself had public-spiritedly taken it away from him and thrown it on top of a cupboard.

The young alibi witnesses did not quite come up to proof. Two boys admitted that there had been a discussion in the witness room about their evidence, and one boy revealed that they had been talking about getting their times right. After two and a half hours of consideration, the jury found Gordon Hay Guilty of murder, although their verdict was not unanimous. Because he had been under 18 at the time of the murder, he was ordered to be detained during Her Majesty's pleasure. An appeal failed. Now Biggar was safe, gossip and suspicion had faded away, boy could meet girl, and the merry-go-round could turn again.

CHAPTER 19
THE ICING ON
THE SHORTBREAD

Ask most husbands how to ice a cake, and they will be mystified. My own husband is no exception. Imagine a middle-aged man in 1906, classic male chauvinist, retired managing director, not well, not calm, an epileptic liable to have a fit at any moment, especially under stress, and aware of that omnipresent possibility, his mind hot and sizzling with mad fancies. Imagine this unsteady figure closeted in a strange bathroom, away from home, struggling to complete an unfamiliar culinary task within the time it would have taken to undress from winter clothing, have a bath, and then re-dress.

With him that morning, concealed about his person, stuffed in the pockets of his overcoat and carried macintosh, there would have been a collection of unwieldy impedimenta: a tin of shortbread, a bag of icing sugar previously or even there and then pounded with crystals of strychnine, a bowl of adequate size, a mixing implement, a spreading implement (perhaps one and the same), brown paper, a gummed label, a card, string and scissors. What finicky foresight would have been required.

At some time, in order to perform the complicated operation of icing the shortbread, he would have had to steal a look at a cookery book. How else could he have possibly known that warm water is the requisite commodity to turn sugar into a runny paste, and that the ratio is half a pound of icing sugar to one to two tablespoons of water? The finished result had to be attractive, appetizing, the lack of commercial smoothness compensated for by the impression that it was home-made, and all the better for it.

What he would not have known was that icing takes an indeterminate time to dry and set, depending upon variables such as the temperature and humidity of the room. A bathroom was the worst place for a quick result. We may fairly expect it to have been hot and steamy. He would have felt impelled to run a bath to sustain the pretence that he was bathing. Since the shortbread tin had to be secreted again for several hours, in the same fashion, the only way to carry it was on its side. If not set, the icing would have run all over the inside of the lid. If he had supported the tin in a horizontal position, at least one of a succession of people who afterwards spent time with him would have noticed the awkward parcel which Mr Brown was clutching so carefully.

Thomas Mathieson Brown, said to be the author of this tricky wizardry, was a pillar of the community, a member of the local school board and a parish councillor, and not at all reclusive, in spite of his disability. He was a chatterbox, even, at times, a windbag. He had views, and he liked to express them. In fact, he should have been admired for his resolve to lead a full life. However, his denial of his illness had, of late, been merging into a lack of insight, an inability to see himself as others saw him. He opened up to people unwisely, and the local sergeant of police, a recipient of his off-beat confidences, had been feeling uneasy about him for quite some time.

Once managing director of the Lanemark Coal Company, until his worsening epilepsy had compelled him to take early retirement in May, 1905, he was, in November, 1906, living in quiet comfort at Ardnith House, New Cumnock, Ayrshire. Although his doctor had advised against wedlock, he had taken a loyal wife 13 years previously, and the marriage, by all accounts, had been happy. There were no children. His best friend was William Lennox – 'Uncle William' – his wife's uncle (she was his favourite niece), who lived at Woodside Cottage, Old Cumnock, five miles away. He was a widower, and kept two servants.

Brown's affliction was no secret: it was impossible to conceal his bizarre symptomatology from the small community. He was widely regarded as weird and unpredictable. Nine years before, when he was working, he had stripped off all his clothes in his office and knelt down at a stool as if to pray. Poor man, the gossip afterwards must have been terrible, although the incident was harmless post-epileptic behaviour about which he would probably have had total amnesia. The epilepsy which had come to dominate his life had been with him for 40 years, since boyhood. The diagnosis was *petit mal*, not the gross convulsions of *grand mal*, but the attacks must have been severe of their kind because Sergeant Harper (the one who kept an eye on him) had twice seen him fall to the ground in a fit.

His GP, Dr Herbertson, had been trying to alleviate his symptoms with bromide since 1880, but the fits had been increasing in intensity and his general mental state was deteriorating. He was usually rational in ordinary conversation, but became boastful and hyperbolic when certain buttons were pushed. His business acumen had deserted him. A number of incorrigible delusions had flowered, so that Brown was by now substantially a chronic insane epileptic. Eagerly he confided to his doctor his conviction that the directors of the railway company were 'on their knees' before him, and that he owned half of Airdrie. A paranoid attitude was beginning to show up: no one in the district knew what was what, except he himself, and he had the power to send one particular man to the gallows and others to prison. Dr Herbertson later said that he would willingly have certified him, if asked to do so, from 1904 onwards. He would have taken action if there had been any complaint that Brown was becoming 'dangerous to the lieges'.

At home, however, unless all his intimates spoke cautiously, the illness was sufficiently masked for those around him to lead reasonably normal lives. His wife found him always kind and quite rational except when the epilepsy came over him. Her sister, Mrs Innes, was happy to visit and stay at Ardnith House with her children. Violet Lambie, the Browns' maid (shades of Helen Lambie, maid to murdered Miss Gilchrist in the Oscar Slater case) had seen some things when her master was ill with the fits: he chased the hens and put them under a box, and pulled up newly-planted flowers by the roots. Mild aberrations these, and, above all, everyone knew that his regard for Uncle William was absolute.

On Monday, November 19th, 1906, Thomas Mathieson Brown rose early, full of plans. The day before, he had told his wife that he would be making one of his trips to Glasgow, to order some goods from Cooper's. As a retired man, it was, no doubt, a struggle to fill in the vacant hours, although his mind was spinning with business notions, which, for some unfathomable reason, were not appreciated by his circle of acquaintances. He had not had a fit for some time and he was in good form as he left for the station, wearing a great-coat and carrying a waterproof – nothing else.

Travelling first-class by the early train, he was soon, by 8.15, presenting himself at the Conservative Club, Bothwell Street and demanding a bath. The hall porter, David Laidlaw, who knew him, took his shilling, thinking that Mr Brown was in a thoughtful mood. He was not carrying anything. No one seems to have asked Laidlaw if Brown regularly took a bath at the club, an indulgence, to kill time. If not, an innocent explanation could be that the early start and the presence of visitors – Mrs Innes and her offspring – had rendered a bath at home inconvenient. No one seems to have asked Laidlaw if there were clear signs that Brown had actually taken a bath when he had vacated the bathroom.

At 9.25am, he was half a mile away, at Cooper's Stores,

Howard Street, where again, he was known. The foreman, Henry Dougal, thought him quite normal as he chatted about the lack of crime in New Cumnock (soon to be remedied) which he attributed to the excellent education offered there. Having ordered some groceries to be sent to St Enoch's Station for the 11.10 train to New Cumnock, he left and vanished from view until he caught the 11.00am express train to Kilmarnock from the same station. He had to be on that train, because, on the Sunday, by post, his wife had arranged a rendezvous for him there with her other sister, Mrs Jessie McCutcheon, who, she knew, was making the same journey. They found each other and chatted of this and that. She noticed that he was carrying a waterproof and a small packet of sweets for the children at home – nothing else.

The train drew in at Kilmarnock at 11.35 and Brown said his goodbyes to his sister-in-law. James Borland, secretary of the Ayrshire Coal Owners' Association, arrived at Kilmarnock Station by train at 11.43. As he left, he met Brown, strolling along from the street in which the post office was situated. He had the air of someone who was just passing the time until his train was due. Chief Constable McHardy later walked the distance at an ordinary pace from the centre of No.4 platform to the post office and it took no more than five minutes. Borland saw that Brown had a coat over his arm, and nothing else. After a few words and a joke – Brown groaned that he had been in the train since one o'clock that morning – he boarded the 11.57 train for New Cumnock, and it steamed out at 11.59. Yet again, he was recognized, this time by William Hastie, colliery manager, who had always found Mr Brown rather taciturn, but this time he could not stop talking. (As an epileptic might react to the stress of the break from routine, the early start, and the strain of having to hold so many conversations.) He even took Hastie back with him for tea at Ardnith House and they discussed business matters. Luncheon seems to have got lost somewhere along the line.

That very Monday evening, crime came to Cumnock. The postman called at Woodside Cottage with a parcel for William Lennox, Esq – so addressed on the label gummed to the brown paper wrapping. Inside, there was a tin box containing a 'cake' of shortbread, rather amateurishly iced. There was an anonymous card, inscribed in pencil, *With happy greetings from an old friend.* The welcome gift was kept abstemiously for the right social occasion, although on the following Thursday the housekeeper, Miss Grace McKerrow, did offer a piece to the maid as a remedy for toothache, on the homeopathic principle, no doubt.

The next evening, Woodside entertained, and the shortbread was triumphantly produced. Mrs Bain, a neighbour, had been invited in. Elizabeth Thorburn, the maid, was given a small piece of the delicacy, as befitted her station in life, and bore it off to gnaw in the kitchen. It was very bitter. She drank some water, but that only made it worse. When she went back to her duties in the parlour, she found the housekeeper white and ill and dizzy, with her body strangely rigid. She warned Elizabeth not to eat any more of the shortbread.

Mrs Bain sent the maid to fetch Dr Robertson and the Murrays, who lived next door. When she returned, the housekeeper was worse, as stiff as a poker and crying out that she had been poisoned. Mrs Bain was feeling ill by now, and Elizabeth supported her home, but she herself was so stiff that she could hardly walk, and had to be helped back herself. William Lennox had been taken ill, but the housekeeper it was that died, not the, as it were, designated victim. Dr Robertson diagnosed that all those stricken were suffering from strychnine poisoning. The others recovered.

There was never any dispute as to the cause of death. Dr McQueen, of Cumnock, conducted a post-mortem, and Professor Harvey Littlejohn found strychnine in the blood, stomach and liver of the deceased. The poison was in the icing, not the shortbread, and there was enough of it left to finish off several people. Very little of the shortbread had been taken from the tin – the dosage had been so severe and the effect so dire and immediate that there had been no opportunity for second helpings. The bitterness had nearly aborted the murderous plan, which had failed, anyway. Poisoners who used the postal method all shared a reckless disregard of the risk that others would be invited or tempted to taste the bait. Peckish Victorian servants in their sunless kitchens were particularly at risk.

The wrapping paper – discovered on the top of the boiler where the housekeeper had stowed it away – together with the label and the card, were preserved for scrutiny. Enquiries were made of chemists and it was soon proved by the poisons register that Thomas Mathieson Brown had purchased one ounce of strychnine from J W Sutherland of Frazer and Green, chemists, Buchanan Street, Glasgow. That was half a year before, on May 2nd, 1906. No more acquisitions of poison were traced to Brown. He told Sutherland that it was for rats, and the chemist, who had supplied him with his bromide for ten years did not doubt him. Later, he foreswore all knowledge of the complaint for which he was dispensing bromide.

Brown's stated purpose for acquiring strychnine was to be soundly ridiculed. His GP, Dr Herbertson, was to testify, although only under cross-examination, that he knew that Brown had bought strychnine on more than one occasion to kill rats, but little notice was taken of this pearl of evidence. Mrs Brown kept hens, and rats were a problem. They always had 'Rough-on-Rats' on hand in the house. She and the maid used to spread the stuff on scones and put them down at the mouth of the rats' holes. The formula for this proprietary rodenticide was barium carbonate and arsenic, lethal enough, one would have thought, but she knew that her husband had poisoned rats of his own accord for years. It was not within her knowledge that he used strychnine.

David Murray, a draper, the next-door neighbour fetched by Elizabeth Thorburn, when all were rigid at Woodside, had conceived a violent dislike and suspicion of Brown, and was to relate what seemed to him to be his sinister, unfeeling and inappropriate behaviour, which heavily told against him. It was the day after the tragedy, when the Browns were visiting Uncle William with their condolences on the death of his housekeeper. Apparently, Brown never looked Murray in the face, never mentioned the death, nor his best friend's frightening illness, and paced the room, prattling about the mineral wealth of New Cumnock and the need for 2,000 new houses to be built. We know that it was his epilepsy that was speaking, but that was nothing to the draper, and he became annoyed and said sharply, 'Mr Brown, death by strychnine is a hell of a death!' whereupon he rushed to the window and complained that 'the machine' (just a car, surely?) was long in coming. As he grew more excited and incoherent he began to boast – nothing on earth had the power to upset him, even if pins were stuck into his body from the crown of his head to the sole of his foot, and he had three bullets in him, put there by North American Indians. This babbling was supposed to be evidential of murderous guilt. Mrs Brown hustled him out of Uncle William's parlour and took him home. She did not let him go to Miss McKerrow's funeral – these occasions could bring on a fit, as could certain colours or even the sight of some people.

Unstable as he undoubtedly was, Thomas Mathieson Brown seemed the ideal suspect and weak links of circumstantial evidence were being forged together. Sergeant Harper came to arrest him on Wednesday, November 28th, when he was playing with the children. His house was searched, and, triumphantly, they found some icing sugar and a small pestle and mortar, in which there was a residue of white powder, but it was harmless and no strychnine whatsoever was traced at Ardnith House by plain means or chemical analysis. The chemist, in May, had told him to dispose of any that he did not use. Violet Lambie, the maid, owned to the icing sugar which she kept in the kitchen press, and none of it, she swore, could have been used without her knowledge. Indeed, a sufficient quantity to ice a cake of shortbread would have made a sizeable reduction in her store of the sugar. Mrs Brown was absolutely sure that her husband could not ice a cake. He took no interest in domestic matters, and she never saw a more helpless man in the kitchen.

The half-baked conjecture of the prosecution was that Brown bought the shortbread on the day and iced it in Glasgow, using a pre-prepared deadly mixture. It would have made more sense if the cake had been one that he had treated previously. There must have been some privacy at Ardnith House. True, no one saw him leave with a parcel, but, equally, no parcel was spotted when he was presumed to have bought the shortbread, first thing in the morning, before he had his bath. Just how big was the 'tin box'? Much was left when four people had taken a polite piece. It had to be large enough to be produced as the pièce de résistance at the little soirée. I think that we can all envisage a typical tin of a flat cake of shortbread and it is not a small object.

Anyway, the provenance of the tin of shortbread was not satisfactorily established. The Crown was pretty sure that it came from the Argyle Street bakery supplied by William Skinner and Sons, Glasgow, but no assistant was brought to identify Brown as a customer early on the Monday morning. George Skinner, manager, was sure that the tin was one of theirs, as was the label, with Skinners' address cut off, and the printed card for messages, and the brown paper wrapping. The 'nipping' around the edge of the cake was 'similar' to that done in their bakery. The icing had been put on by an unskilled hand. He had no reason to doubt that the cake had been made by his firm.

But wait! The man on the shop floor, James Moir, foreman baker, thought that, judging by the 'nipping', it was *not* a Skinners' cake. Is he suggesting that some skilled hand packed a counterfeit cake into a Skinners' box? He seemed happy enough that it was a Skinners' box, since none of the firm's rivals used boxes of that pattern. And then, his colleague, the foreman confectioner, could not say if it was verily a Skinners' cake.

A ludicrous attempt was made to place Brown at the bakery. Euphemia Glass, manageress, produced the ribbons used in the cash register early on the Monday. The fourth entry showed a sale to the value of 2s 4d. The price of a tin of shortbread of the relevant type was 2s 3d. A penny-worth of sweets, it was suggested, could account for the rounding-up. One would think that the fourth customer of the day could feasibly have been memorable. If Euphemia Glass had witnessed Brown in mid-transaction, demanding wrapping materials, that would have been a different proposition. Anyway, the sweets were not seen by anyone until he was on the express train. He could just as well have bought them at Cooper's, or elsewhere.

No one saw Brown in the Kilmarnock post office, either. The postal markings on the killing parcel showed beyond a doubt that someone had posted it from there on the morning of Brown's trip to town. Unhappily for the Crown, however, all the clerical staff at the post office stated that the markings showed that it must have been posted before 11.30am. William Dixon, chief porter at Kilmarnock Station, indubitably the right man to ask, swore that Brown's 11.00am express from Glasgow arrived precisely at 11.30am.

The only direct evidence against Brown (and the trial judge is my authority here) was that relating to the handwriting on the label and the card. It was admitted by those defending him that there was an unfortunate resemblance between Brown's handwriting and that on the label. The Crown brought two expert witnesses, an engraver and a lithographic writer, to say that he had, indeed written the label, and also the card, although in that latter case he had disguised his hand. The defence relied on a single, impressive witness, Dr Birch, handwriting expert at the British Museum, who opined that it was impossible to state that the label, the card, and specimen letters written by Brown were all in the same hand. The writing on the card was upright, that on the card backhanded, and it would not be safe to assume that one person was responsible for both. However, Peter Dowie, Secretary of the Lanemark Coal Company, who knew Brown intimately, was certain that he had written the label. He could not say if he had written the message on the card. If it were his work, it was in a disguised hand.

Brown was incarcerated at Ayr, and, because of his known psychiatric history, two alienists – Dr John Carswell, Certifying Surgeon in Lunacy to the Glasgow Parish Council, and Donald Fraser, MO, Riccartsbrae Lunatic Asylum, Paisley, were brought in to examine him. They were admirably thorough, seeing him four or five times in all. So dark was their view of his mental state that he seems to bear small resemblance to the respectable husband and citizen, playing with the children at home and dealing with the shopkeepers of Glasgow.

Dr Carswell observed that Brown's general aspect was excitable and impulsive – which would seem to be quite appropriate, since he knew that he was already indicted for the murder of Miss McKerrow – and that he saw everything from an unreal point of view, with his mental processes distorted. The case was absolutely incurable. Later, the doctor told the court that one of the most common influences contributing towards homicidal impulses was the fury that occurred in connection with epileptic attacks. No doubt, but epileptic furore simply does not explain the preparation and despatch of the poisoned cake, a project which was so conspicuously premeditated. There was no fit around the operative time, and we have to look to Brown's delusional areas for a morbid motive for attempting to murder his best friend. No paranoid thoughts about Uncle William were ever elicited or surfaced spontaneously. All of those close to him stressed his normal and humane reaction to the death. William Lennox himself said that Brown seemed very sorry about what had happened, which contradicts Murray the draper's impression.

The two doctors certified that Thomas Mathieson Brown was of unsound mind and not capable of pleading to the indictment. However, Brown strongly desired to plead Not Guilty and his law agent and counsel supported his wish to have a trial. On March 18th, 1907, his case was duly heard, but the jury returned a majority verdict that he was insane at the time of trial, and he was borne off to the fate which he had most shunned – to be a 'Pleasure man' at the Criminal Lunatic Department, Perth. Not unlike our modern Dr Shipman, he was described as a quiet, respectable-looking man of middle-age, who 'presented no appearance of mental aberration except that he wore a beard'. He plainly conducted himself well in confinement, being conditionally released in May, 1907, when he was removed to the Crichton Royal Institution, Dumfries. He died at Ayr County Asylum.

Brown's case appears in Scottish law books, illustrating the principle that although the result of the act done may not be that which was intended, the perpetrator may still be guilty of a criminal act. Real doubts remain. The crystals of strychnine in the icing on the shortbread were found by the Edinburgh city analyst to be very small, and much smaller than those in the strychnine bought by Brown six months earlier. This assumes that he had kept and used precisely that supply for his murderous purpose. It was suggested that he pounded up the strychnine in a mortar and thereby reduced the size of the crystals. But can crystals be reduced in this way? My researches have shown experts to be divided on this crucial point.

Is it possible that a killer from Kilmarnock, man or woman, motivated by some old grudge, as in a Sherlock Holmes mystery, or driven by outright insanity, posted the poisoned parcel, and that it was coincidental that Brown was out and about on the same day? It was too easy to blame the neighbourhood epileptic who actually knew the intended victim. Prejudice was at work.